D# 267044

D0796696

RICKS COLLEGE
DAVID O. McKAY LIBRARY
REXBURG, IDAHO 83440

WITHDRAWN

F 1 0 2023

The Villanelle
The Evolution of a Poetic Form

FEB 1 0 2013

The Villanelle

The Evolution of a Poetic Form

Ronald E. McFarland

The University of Idaho Press
Moscow, Idaho

Published by The University of Idaho Press
Moscow, Idaho 83843
(c) 1987 by Ronald E. McFarland
Design by Melissa Rockwood
All rights reserved.
Printed in the United States of America
9 8 7 6 5 4 3 2 1

The following journals have generously given permission to adapt
for use herein articles published originally under their auspices:
Italian Quarterly, for "The Italian Villanella and the Problems of
'Popular Art'," 22 (Summer 1981):15–29; *Romanic Review*, for
"The Revival of a 'Poetical Trifle'," 73 (March 1982): 167–183;
Victorian Poetry, for "The Villanelle in English, 1874–1922," 20
(Summer 1982):125–138; and *Modern Poetry Studies*, for "The Form
and its Transformation in Contemporary Poetry," 11(1982):
113–127.

Library of Congress Cataloging-in-Publication Data

McFarland, Ronald E.
      The villanelle : the evolution of a poetic form / Ronald E.
McFarland.
          p. cm.
      Includes bibliographical references and index.
      ISBN 0-89301-121-5
      1. English poetry—History and criticism. 2. Villanelles—
History and criticism. 3. English poetry—European influences.
4. Romance poetry—History and criticism. 5. Literary form.
6. Literature, Comparative—English and Romance. 7. Literature, Comparative—Romance and English. I. Title
PR509.V54M36 1987
809.1—dc19   87-24136
                                                                   CIP

ISBN 0-89301-121-5

For my parents

Contents

Preface

"*I*t's all a trick," W. W. Skeat, the noted medievalist, once said of the villanelle in a villanelle of his own, "As easy as reciting ABC."* He argues, quite persuasively in a way, that "You need not be an atom of a poet" to write a villanelle. Quite a number of villanelles have been and are being written by recipe, and if one were to judge the form by those poems, one might agree with Skeat's thesis. Playwright Eugene O'Neill's playful villanelles are perhaps justly consigned to oblivion. Novelist John Updike's "Energy: A Villanelle," published in the *New Yorker* (4 June 1979, p. 44) is at least more in earnest, but no one reading it would advise him to give up fiction for poetry. For the poet, the form is not so much a "trick" as a challenge. I hope this book will demonstrate, among other things, that while it is indeed easy to write a villanelle, it is not so easy to write a good villanelle, and that a good villanelle, like any other good poem, results from a fortunate fusion of content and form. Too often critics and scholars are inclined to emphasize content and form rather than that which is "fortunate"—the luck, inspiration, or craft of the poet—as if content, and more especially form, were pulled from some universal shelf accessible alike to critic, scholar, and poet. In short, the villanelle does not make the poet; the poet makes the villanelle.

In the present age of free verse and "open-form" poetry, an age which, neglecting Walt Whitman, has had continuous existence now for seventy-odd years, the villanelle may seem either an anachronism or a peculiarity. Undeniably, modern poets have tried the villanelle merely to demonstrate, perhaps to themselves as much as to their readers, that they can write not only conventional accentual–syllabic verse, but also that they have so mastered the craft that they can write a good poem in one of the most demanding of all conventional forms. And just as the challenge presented by the sonnet is in part a matter of language, of assimilating a form devised for a Romance language (Italian) into English, so is the challenge of the villanelle one of finding in English the resources to handle a form designed for French. But probably because ours is an age of conscious formlessness on the one hand, or of subtle, one is

---

* William Cole, ed., *The Fireside Book of Humorous Poetry* (New York: Simon and Schuster, 1959):441.

tempted to say "formless," form on the other, twentieth-century poets have modified the villanelle in various ways. Experimenters have produced some exceptionally powerful poems, even as close adherents to the form have brought the villanelle in English to a high level. The thoroughbreds coexist with the hybrids.

Very few writers of the villanelle in English are aware of its complete history any more than I was when I began research into the subject. Many poets have been influenced only by direct predecessors who have written villanelles in English. Some have been aware of various French antecedents, usually limited to Jean Passerat. Few, however, have known of its Italian origins. While the primary intent of this book is to examine the development of achievements in the form by English and American poets, I have devoted almost half of it to the history of the villanelle in Italian and French poetry. The result is a literary history of sorts, as well as a formalistic and generic study.

Throughout, I have not hesitated to quote the entire texts of poems. It seems to me that this is a major advantage the student of lyric poetry has over students of other genres. Moreover, with the notable exceptions of Dylan Thomas's "Do Not Go Gentle into that Good Night" and Theodore Roethke's "The Waking," the villanelles discussed herein are not generally known, and many are not readily accessible. If the result is a sort of anthology with running commentary, I cannot offer a very sincere apology, for I have not intended anything so imposing as to show the villanelle the equal of the sonnet, the "Great Metric Hope," or the last net across Robert Frost's tennis court.

In fact, I have gone so far as to append a small anthology of villanelles by contemporary poets, some of whom are unknown and may remain that way. This last section of the book is like the last paragraph of an essay, in that it anticipates the future of the subject. Philip K. Jason's essay in *College Literature* 7 (Spring 1980) may have aroused some fresh interest in the villanelle, and short sequences and collections of villanelles have been published in the past several years, but I do not expect a spate of them to rival the rage for the sonnet during the late Renaissance. The villanelle has, however, escaped the nearly automatic triviality of its early application in English and in many French poems. Trivial poets will always exist, though, and they will turn to the villanelle on occasion. The form does lend itself to sometimes delightful comic uses. If nothing else, I hope this study proves its flexibility, even when the poems are composed according to the strictest rules.

♦♦♦

Acknowledgments are gratefully made for permission to reprint the following in the anthology of contemporary villanelles with which this volume concludes: Elizabeth Bishop, "One Art," *Geography III* (New York: Farrar, Straus & Giroux, 1976); Imogene L. Bolls, "Dying is a Matter of Degrees," *Mississippi Review* 4 (1975); Harold Bond, "Krumple the Landlord," *Ararat* (Spring 1971); Joanna Cattonar, "Sand Creek," (permission of the author); Ann Fox Chandonnet, "If Our Minds Mated as Our Bodies Do," *Black Sun, New Moon* (Chapel Hill, NC: Carolina Wren Press, 1980); Philip Dacey, "A Walk in the Country," *Plains Poetry Journal* (1982); Madeline DeFrees, "Keeping Up with the Signs," *Magpie on the Gallows* (Port Townsend, WA: Copper Canyon Press, 1982); Marilyn Folkestad, "Maggie," *Snapdragon* 2 (Spring 1979):63; Charles Guenther, "Missouri Woods," *Webster Review* 1 (Summer 1974):13; Annette Hayn, "The Way You Are," *Light* 1 (1974); Edward Harkness, "The Man in the Recreation Room," *Long Eye Lost Wind Forgive Me* (Copperhead Press, 1975); Bonnie Hirsch, "Planting Cacti in Jars Saved from the Farm Dump," *Eight Idaho Poets* (Moscow, ID: The University of Idaho Press, 1979); Rolfe Humphries, "Runes for an Old Believer" *Collected Poems* (Bloomington: Indiana University Press, 1965); Phyllis Janowitz, "Wilbur," *Rites of Strangers* (Charlottesville: University of Virginia Press, 1978); George Keithley, "If April," (revised) *Three Rivers Poetry Journal* 17/18 (1981):28; Carolyn Kizer, "On a Line from Sophocles," *Midnight Was My Cry* (Garden City, NY: Doubleday, 1971); Barbara Lefcowitz, "Home Movies," *A Risk of Green* (Gallimaufry Press, 1978), and "Rerun Berries: A Prose Villanelle" (permission of the author); Norman N. McWhinney, "Truth Lies in Paradox," *Truth Lies in Paradox: Sonnets and Villanelles* (Derry, PA: Rook Press, 1977):27; Christopher Millis, "Ceremony," *Cutbank* 26 (Spring/Summer 1980:16; Howard Nemerov, "Equations of a Villanelle," *The Western Approaches* (Chicago: University of Chicago Press, 1975 and by permission of the author); William Packard, "The Teacher of Poetry," *First Selected Poems* (New York: Pylon Press, 1977):37; Henry Petroski, "Self-Portrait," *Southern Humanities Review* (Spring 1971); Alberto Ríos, "La Sequía/The Drought," *Waters*; Helen Saslow, "Villanelle: Night Watch," *Glassworks* 3 (1977–78); Kim Stafford, "Villanelle for the Spiders," *A Gypsy's History of the World* (Port Townsend, WA: Copper Canyon Press, 1976); David Wagoner, "Canticle for Xmas Eve," *First Light* (Boston: Atlantic-Little, Brown, 1983):56; John Wain, "Villanelle: For Harpo Marx" (permission of the author); Jeanne Murray Walker, "Villanelle to Wake My Love," *Arizona Quarterly* 33 (Spring 1977):86; Celeste Turner Wright, "Reprieve," *California Quarterly* (1981); Charles David Wright, "Wearing Well," *Early Rising* (Chapel Hill: University of North Carolina Press, 1968); Harald Wyndham, "Villanelle: The Dying Man," *Eight Idaho Poets* (Moscow, ID: University of Idaho Press, 1979):30.

◆◆◆

I am grateful to the University of Idaho for a sabbatical leave and for a summer research grant, without which aid this book would have been a fond impossibility. In addition to harrassing the interlibrary loan staff for over a year, I have been permitted to use the facilities of the Huntington Library in San Marino, California, and the libraries at the University of Washington, University of Michigan, the University of California at Los Angeles and at Berkeley, and the University of Oregon. Many individuals have been especially helpful along the way: Professors Winfried and Louise Schleiner of Davis, California, Dody Dozier of Moscow, Idaho, and many poets who responded to my requests for the contributions and comments on the villanelle. Finally, I would like to express my gratitude to my long-suffering wife and family— Elsie, Kimberley, Jennifer, and Jonathan.

Do Not Go Gentle into that Good Night

Do not go gentle into that good night,
Old age should burn and rave at close of day;
Rage, rage against the dying of the light.

Though wise men at their end know dark is right,
Because their words had forked no lightning they
Do not go gentle into that good night.

Good men, the last wave by, crying how bright
Their frail deeds might have danced in a green bay,
Rage, rage against the dying of the light.

Wild men who caught and sang the sun in flight,
And learn, too late, they grieved it on its way,
Do not go gentle into that good night.

Grave men, near death, who see with blinding sight
Blind eyes could blaze like meteors and be gay,
Rage, rage against the dying of the light.

And you, my father, there on the sad height,
Curse, bless, me now with your fierce tears, I pray.
Do not go gentle into that good night.
Rage, rage against the dying of the light.

                                          Dylan Thomas

The Waking

I wake to sleep, and take my waking slow.
I feel my fate in what I cannot fear.
I learn by going where I have to go.

We think by feeling. What is there to know?
I hear my being dance from ear to ear.
I wake to sleep, and take my waking slow.

Of those so close beside me, which are you?
God bless the Ground! I shall walk softly there,
And learn by going where I have to go.

Light takes the Tree; but who can tell us how?
The lowly worm climbs up a winding stair;
I wake to sleep, and take my waking slow.

Great Nature has another thing to do
To you and me; so take the lively air,
And, lovely, learn by going where to go.

This shaking keeps me steady. I should know.
What falls away is always. And is near.
I wake to sleep, and take my waking slow.
I learn by going where I have to go.

                                        Theodore Roethke

1.
The Italian Villanella and the Problems of "Popular Art"

*A*lthough Jean Passerat's "J'ai perdu ma tourterelle," the paradigm for the villanelle in French and English poetry since it was taken up in the mid-nineteenth century, is the embodiment of sophisticated artifice, the origins of the form appear to have been in popular poetry. The Italian, or Neapolitan, villanella of sixteenth-century vocal music, however, familiar through the settings of such composers as Adrian Willaert and Luca Marenzio, are related to the courtly madrigal rather than to popular song. Consider, moreover, the conventional conceit in the following villanella from Giovanni Zappasorgo's *Napolitane* (1578):

> Amor m'ha desfidato alla battaglia
> La fronte di Madonna sará il campo
> E temo e spero et ardo e non ho scampo.
> I bei capelli d'or faran la corda,
> E li sguardi saette, i cigli gl'archi,
> Gl'occhi lucenti archibugetti carchi.
> Io posto per trombetta alti sospiri,
> Humilitá per impresa, et ella altiera
> Ha l'arme nude, e sdegnha la bandiera.
> Spuntando il Sol cominciarem l'assalto,
> Benche alla donna mia leggiadra e audace
> Mi renderò gridando pace pace.[1]

The extended battle metaphor, though not complex and certainly not inventive, is nevertheless the work of a sophisticated poet well aware of the Petrarchan tradition and its conventions. The poem is far from any "primitive" or "folk" source, and it may be wondered whether the designation "popular" is in any sense justified.

The ostensible popularity of the villanella has never been established, even though the issue has been a part of Italian scholarship and criticism since the late nineteenth century. Although he was essentially committed to promoting the popular basis of the form in his extensive study, *Le Villanelle* (1925), Gennaro Maria Monti was compelled to observe that it was both popular and courtly at once.[2] Feeling that Monti had argued too forcefully in favor of the popular origins of the villanella in Neapolitan dialect poems, Carlo Calcaterra warned that the form must not be regarded as in any sense the work of a folk poet.[3] Bianca Maria Galanti's more recent study asserts that the villanella is an artistic composition derived from folk or popular materials (i.e., *materia villanesca*).[4]

One reason why the question of the villanella's popular status is difficult to resolve is that the term "villanella" is not clearly associated with the genre until the publication of the *Canzone villanesche alla napolitana* in 1537. The assumption has been that the composers of those settings worked from an already existing body of popular poetry, and this assumption would appear to be correct. Within four years of the first anonymous collection of villanelle, Giovanni da Nola's *Canzone villanesche* was published in Venice, inaugurating a host of song books by such noted musicians as Perissone, Willaert, and Lasso. By 1555 the villanella had crossed the Alps, Orlando di Lasso's collection having been published in Antwerp. In short, the rapid ascent of the villanella after publication of the 1537 volume would suggest that a body of popular villanelle already existed, whether Neapolitan or more generally distributed throughout Italy. Calcaterra implies that this is the case, and the noted musicologist, Alfred Einstein, is able to date a *comedia a la vilanescha* early in 1520.[5] Once the song books came into vogue, of course, there was considerable composition of *poesia per musica*. Since most of the villanelle are anonymous, it is virtually impossible to be certain which poems were written specifically for the composers (and sometimes by the composers) in imitation of the preexisting, presumably popular poems.

The Italian villanelle which I will examine hereafter assume a popular tone for the most part, as Galanti has indicated, but usually with a certain affectation of *concetti*, refinement of sentiment, and preciseness of phrasing and versification that will cause us to regard the sixteenth-century product as a sophisticated adaptation of an earlier and more genuinely popular, or even folk, form of poetry.[6]

Some sense of what that earlier form of poetry may have been like can be seen, I would like to hypothesize, in the Spanish "villancico."

Except for the etymological connection, little similarity between the forms has been demonstrated. Spanish scholars have preferred to see the villancico as a native form, perhaps related to the Moorish (Mozarabic) *zéjel* or even to the Gallician–Portuguese *cantiga de amigo*, while Italian scholars tend to see the villanella as a native offshoot of the "frottola," at least as a type of song. As Monti has observed, however, there was a flowering of such "materia rusticale" throughout Spain, Portugal, and Italy in the sixteenth century.[7] In his study of the villancico Antonio Sánchez Romeralo goes so far as to speculate on the possibility of an early impulse from the Spanish court of Alfonso V in Naples.[8] Whether the courtiers of Aragon carried home a native Italian song (perhaps similar to that already in existence in Spain), or whether they brought an even earlier Mozarabic tradition with them to Naples during Alfonso's reign (1443–1458), it is the Spanish villancico that offers the earliest materials for a study of villanesche ("villano"-peasant) poetry as a popular lyric.

Following the general structure of the tenth- and eleventh-century zéjel, the villancico of the mid-fifteenth century is composed of a short (two to four lines) *estribillo*, or refrain, which announces the subject or theme of the poem; a midsection of variable length (early villancicos often just four lines, but twenty or more at the hands of such poets as Manuel Jiménez de Urrea) called the *mudanza*, or change; and a brief return, the *vuelta*, which unites the mudanza with the estribillo.[9] The particular appeal of the early villancicos is their simplicity. The example below, I think, is not very distant from certain types of folk song.

> Vésame y abràcame
>   Marido mio,
> Y daros en la mañana
>   Camisòn limpio.
> Yo nunca vi hombre
> Bivo estar tan muerto,
> Ni hazer el dormido
> Estando despierto.
> Andad marido alerta
>   Y tened brio,
> Y daros en la mañana,
>   Camisòn limpio.[10]

In this poem there is no trace of Petrarchism (a significant influence in Spanish poetry by this date), either in theme or in language. As is fairly often the case in the villancico, the speaker is a woman, and the humor is broad and genuinely playful. The language of the poem is illustrative of the qualities which Romeralo has isolated as typical of popular poetry, among which are: dynamic expression through the predominance of verbs concerning physical activity; scarcity of qualifying adjectives and adverbs; lack of hyperbolic statement. The line is typically short, unlike the predominant hendecasyllables of the villanella, and there are no effusive emotions of the sort which characterize later "cultivated" villancicos and villanelle.

The earliest villancicos, dating prior to 1445, are no more than two- or three-line estribillos without elaboration. I offer two examples from the fifteenth century:

> La ninya que los amores ha,
> ¿como dormira sola?

> (Romeralo, p. 391)

> Aquel caballero, madre,
> tres besicos le mandé;
> creceré y dárselos he.

> (Romeralo, p. 392)

The second of the examples illustrates Romeralo's observation that in the popular, as opposed to the cultivated or sophisticated villancico, the confidante of the speaker is not birds or trees, but the mother: "La madre es, así, realmente, la única confidente del villancico:" (p. 265). Such realistic details contribute to the popular character of the villancico.

To these simple, popular estribillos more sophisticated poets added *glosas* which constituted a considerable elaboration of the form, rendering it of interest to such poets as Juan del Encina, Lope de Vega, Santa Teresa de Jesús, Cervantes, Tirso de Molina, Góngora, indeed to nearly every major poet of the Spanish Renaissance and Golden Age (Romeralo, pp. 84-5). One of the best known of the anonymous villancicos is the one below:

> Tres morillas me enamoran
> en Jaén:
> Axa y Fátima y Marién.

> Tres morillas tan garridas
> iban a coger olivas;
> y hallábanlas cogidas
> en Jaén:

Axa y Fátima y Marién.
Y hallábanlas cogidas;
y tornaban desmaidas
y las colores perdidas,
en Jaén:
Axa y Fátima y Marién.

Tres moricas tan lozanas,
tres moricas tan lozanas
iban a coger manzanas
a Jaén:
Axa y Fátima y Marién.

(Romeralo, p. 396)

The truncated second line of the estribillo and the rhyme scheme (*abb*) are common to the form. As Gerald Brenan observes, songs like this one "were clearly meant for the open air."[11] The subject matter, Brenan indicates, is from an ancient Arabic poem which related with indecent language a scandal that had taken place in the harem of Harun al-Raschid (caliph of Baghdad, 786–809). Once the estribillo began to function simply as an introductory stanza, the cultivated or sophisticated villancico was born, but its popular character was lost. As with the villanella, the villancico was set to music for chamber recital, but it never achieved the popularity in Europe of the Italian villanella (for obvious reasons, given the politics of the day and the status of Italian musicians). Later in the sixteenth century the villancico became a staple of Christmas recitals and was performed, often by choirs from cathedral schools, on Christmas Eve. The nativity villancicos retained their popularity well into the eighteenth century, and the term is now commonly used to designate the "Christmas carol."

Although we may be reasonably confident that the villancico was at one time actually popular in nature (literally "of the people") and perhaps had its origins in folk poetry, we might be justifiably less confident about the villanella. In fact, I cannot demonstrate for the villanella what Romeralo has been able to find for the villancico, and it is primarily for that reason that I have spent some time on the Spanish form, the influence of which does not appear to have been felt in France. The pervasive influence of Petrarch is, I think, the single factor that has most compromised the popular character of the villanella. In examining the Italian villanella we shall look for traces of an earlier period when the form may have been transcribed from the voices of nonliterate singers, or when it was written by popular poets who were unaware of or impervious to the conventions favored by sophisticated or courtly Italian poets. As Galanti has noted, however, agreeing with Benedetto Croce, the major difference between "poesia d'arte" and "poesia popolare" is in the "psychological tone" of the poem, and ultimately, of course, of the poet (p. xxiv). It will not do to argue that an anonymous poem is *ipso facto* popular, or that a poem in Neapolitan dialect is necessarily popular, or even that a poem about rustic or village life is popular. Finally, no metrical scheme, even though it may be very simple, and even though the use of repetition and refrain has been shown to be basic to primitive song, can be classified as popular. A popular poem is one which, whether written or not, is sustained by the people. The most we can say of the sixteenth-century villanelle which we are about to examine is that, in general, they may derive from poems or songs that once were popular. They may possess, therefore, a certain popular tone in addition to the more obvious elements of popular poetry which are being imitated, such as a marketplace setting, characters drawn from the laboring classes or peasantry, coarse diction, or certain metrical forms.

At least as important as assessing the presumed popularity of the villanella, however, is the task of defining its characteristics and then of evaluating some of the poems for their literary merits. Unlike the villancico, the villanella does not appear to have attracted the major Italian poets of the sixteenth and seventeenth centuries. There are exceptions, like Giovan Leone Sempronio's (1603–46) "Ballo di villanelle,"[12] but there are far more instances like that of Tasso, among whose hundreds of sonnets, madrigals, and ballatas is to be found not a single villanella.

G. M. Monti's definition of the villanella has been generally accepted by subsequent scholars. Any consideration of the genre ought properly, therefore, to begin with his statement that the villanelle is "un componimento lirico composto di distici a rima baciata distribuiti in strofe eguali per ampiezza e distribuzione di rime e di metri, i quali distici, alcune volte, sono preceduti o seguiti da uno o più versi liberi, altre volte no. In alcuni casi, vi sono legami tra le strofe oppure v'è il ritornello, per la maggior parte le strofe sono indipendenti l'una dall'altra. Mancano del tutto le rime alternate (ABAB) e le rime incrociate (ABBA)" (pp. 47–8). Obviously, Monti's definition is limited to the formal characteristics of the villanella. The reason for this, as will soon be apparent, is that the subject matter and the thematic range of the form are virtually unlimited. It cannot even be argued that there is a tone or attitude peculiar to the villanella. In that direction, the most one can say is that the subject of romantic love is nearly universal to the villanella, that the Petrarchan themes predominate, and that the tones and attitudes are also conventionally Petrarchan. The various exceptions to these statements are not sufficient to require more than the qualifications that I have already made.

As Monti demonstrates, the stanza length and the line length of the villanella vary considerably, though there are some general tendencies. The eleven-syllable (hendecasyllabic) line is most common, and four stanzas is the most frequent length for the poems. Moreover, two strophic types appear more than any others, type A^1 (quatrains rhyming *aabb, ccdd,* etc.) and type B^1 (tercets composed of a distich with a free line, thus *abb, cdd,* etc.). Of more than seven hundred villanelle examined, more than one-fourth were of type A^1 and more than a fourth were of type B^1 (pp. 49–52). Among the other variations, Monti found only one other scheme to be widespread. Over fifty villanelle were of type IVe, which shows singularity of rhyme pattern in the fourth stanza and involves minimal variation of rhyme in the tercets (thus, *abb, abb, abb, ccc,* the second b-rhyme often being a refrain line). This pattern is related to the strambotto form (*abababcc*), forerunner of ottava rima. Monti describes the IVe pattern as "specie tra le villanelle più antiche a più dialettali" (p. 61). This type, and to a lesser extent type B^1, shows considerable similarities to the tercet form of Passerat: $A^1bA^2, abA^1, abA^2, abA^1, abA^2, abA^1A^2$. As I have already noted, the estribillo in the Spanish villancico is often written on the *abb* pattern, but the similarity may be no more than coincidence. Mario Menghini's early study of one hundred fifty-three villanelle in the Chigiano codex (L, IV, 81) includes fifty-eight poems in tercets, twelve of which are on the *ab*B scheme. Alfredo Obertello's more recent examination of twenty-nine villanelle published in England during the sixteenth century includes eighteen in tercet form, eleven of which are of the *ab*B pattern.[13]

The example below of a villanella in the *ab*B scheme (set by Orlando di Lasso) illustrates once again the permeation of Petrarchan diction, imagery, and theme.

> Tu sai, Madonna mia, ch'io t'am' e voglio
> Tanto di ben ch'io non ritrovo loco;

Perchè prendete l'mio martir in gioco?

Se sai che del tuo laccio mai mi scioglio
Et per voi me nutrico in fiamma e foco,
Perchè prendete l'mio martir in gioco?

Se sai che la mia fede è fermo scoglio
Che per voi mi consumo a poco a poco,
Perchè prendete l'mio martir in gioco?

Dunque, madonna, cessa il tuo furore,
Abbi pietà de chi t'ha dato il core
Ch'in vita e morte t'è bon servitore![14]

There are two basic Petrarchan situations to which nearly all other contexts are related. Either the lover praises the beauty of his beloved, lamenting or complaining of his condition, which arises from the disdain or indifference which accompanies that beauty; or he laments or complains about his condition, which is a result of her disdain or indifference. While this might appear to be a distinction without a difference, the strategies underlying the approaches are quite different. In the first case, the speaker attempts to flatter his mistress, thus disarming her at least until he yields to his own misfortunes. In the second, as in the poem above, the speaker is the actual subject of the poem, which is primarily intended as a proclamation of love and fidelity in the face of adversity. In both cases, of course, the mistress is assailed for her cruelty. (In poems addressed to Love, the approach is usually the same: either the mistress's beauty and disdain are central to the poem, or the lover's agony.) The logical structure of "Tu sai, Madonna" suggests that it is a product of the "Musa dotta" (Monti, p. 244) rather than of the "labbra del popolo": "Tu sai, Madonna . . . Perchè, prendete . . . ; Se sai che. . . Perchè prendete . . . ; Se sai che . . . Perchè prendete . . . ; Dunque, madonna. . . . " The imagery of bindings, flames, and (implicitly) the sea wearing on the steadfast reef are as conventional as the ideas, though whether this relates the poem to the people or to the court would be impossible to say. Surely, however, the poet is sophisticated. In addition to the logical play in the structure of the poem, he also indulges in some interesting compounding of diction in each stanza: am'e voglio, fiamma e foco, a poco a poco, vita e morte. The result of such sophisticated artifice is not necessarily good poetry. In this case, in fact, the final impression is of a sort of glibness that one might associate with *poesia per musica*.

Monti traces the descent of the villanella from the thirteenth-century Neapolitan *mattinata* (morning song) and finds the dialect poems of such poets as "Sbruffapappa," Velardiniello, and Giovanni della Carriola to be the most genuinely popular. I will take an example of the popular type, not in Neapolitan dialect, comparable in some ways to the poem just cited, from Monti (p. 163).

> Tutti amano le donne che son belle
> et io le voglio che mi voglion bene,
> e dello resto come vene vene.
>
> Chi la vuol bianca e chi la vuol brunetta,
> e chi magra, e chi grassa, e chi verace;
> et a me l'una come l'altra piace.
>
> Chi la vuol vedovella, e chi citella,
> chi la vuol maritata, e chi matrona,
> et a me l'una e l'altra me sa buona.
>
> Ma per dir chiara la mia fantasia,
> io che n'aggio vedute de più sorte,
> la villanella mi da vita e morte!

As with "Tu sai, Madonna," this villanella is composed of four tercets in hendecasyllabic lines. The rhyme scheme is the more common B^1 type described by Monti. The speaker, however, is closer to the tradition of Donne's "The Indifferent," "I can love both fair and brown," than he is to the Petrarchan lover. The problem, however, is that the speaker in this poem is no less conventional than the one in "Tu sai, Madonna." Moreover, while this poem lacks the tight logical structure of the former, the sophisticated play of balance and parallelism throughout (notably in the construction of the second and third tercets) and the consistent use of the third line for witty contradictions should warn us that the poet is by no means a simple street-singer. The concluding line, though it is one of the few moments in which the speaker might appear to be popular (since he prefers the "villanella," or country-peasant maiden), actually returns us to a Petrarchan vision ("vita e morte") similar to that of "Tu sai, Madonna." It is perhaps for this reason that Menghini describes the villanella as "una forma della poesia *semipopolare* italiana" (p. 477, italics mine).

In writing on the poetic qualities of the villanella, Monti begins by observing that the popular and the courtly come together: "musa popolare e musa aulica s'incontrano di continuo, s'intrecciano, si scambiano immagini" (p. 219). Nevertheless, he attempts to distinguish what might be called the popular "strains" from the courtly. Unfortunately, his criteria are not as carefully defined as those in Romeralo's study of the villancico. At one place Monti characterizes the popular style as "spigliato" (easy) and syntactically uncomplicated, with imagery that is usually marked by "un valore di schiettezza e di soavità" (p. 170). Elsewhere, he notes the great difference between "la spontaneità" of the popular manner and "l'artifizio" of the courtly (p. 225). The distinctions between the popular and courtly styles, therefore, remain uncertain and largely a matter of subjective judgment in Monti's account.

Perhaps the matter deserves some reconsideration before we turn to the examination of some representative villanelle. The inclination of literary critics is to ascribe to popular poetry such values as freshness of imagery, simplicity of theme, ease of language and syntax, and infrequent use of conventional rhetorical devices. Those who read the popular poetry of any age, however, will discover that whether the poet is George Wither, Robert Service, Edgar Guest, or Rod McKuen, what typifies his work is the attempt to sound or appear "poetical." Every era produces thousands of such poets, some more successful than others, most of whom waste their sweetness on the desert air (and thank God for that). The qualities thought by some to be popular are in fact more appropriate to what C. M. Bowra terms "primitive" poetry. Such familiar medieval lyrics as "Sumer is Icumen In," which might be designated "folk" or "primitive," are close to the Native American and aboriginal verse that Bowra deals with and are probably deserving of such descriptions as easy, fresh, and spontaneous.[15] At the opposite extreme of the continuum (the categories can not be thought of as exclusive or altogether distinct) is sophisticated poetry, what is now called "serious" and was in sixteenth-century Italy the poetry of the court. The sophisticated or serious poet writes from a tradition in which he is attempting to establish a unique voice. In this effort he may use the equipment (conventions) of that tradition, or he may rebel against it. But the important thing is that he is aware of it and is working through it to establish an individual style. Popular poetry, properly speaking, falls somewhat uncomfortably between these extremes. This is especially true of the Italian villanella.

The reason the popular poet avoids sophisticated artifice is, presumably, that he chooses to direct his poems toward an audience that could not comprehend or approve eccentricities of style and theme. He prefers to appear familiar, however, and so clings fairly closely to convention. He must satisfy a generally conservative public taste in order to prove that he is writing legitimate poetry. In sixteenth-century Italy such a writer might draw from Petrarchan lore, but he might be cautious in his use of mythology. An allusion to theft or to a trial might be accessible to his reader, while a metaphor involving technical legal terms would almost certainly err against the decorum of popular poetics. The popular poet's range of vocabulary, metaphor, and allusion, therefore, is severely curtailed. In many ways the task of the popular poet is considerably harder than that of the courtly or sophisticated poet, who may indulge himself pretty much at will. His task is also more difficult than that of the folk poet, whose conventions are rooted in the community and often in religious ceremony. The many anonymous writers of the Italian villanella—and there are no "masters" of the form—generally produce a sort of poem which may be termed "popular" along the lines here indicated.

The subject matter and themes of the villanella are conventional and generally Petrarchan. The speaker is almost always a male, whose beautiful but cruel mistress has spurned him or treated him with indifference. In his plight, confused by the discrepancy between the woman's physical beauty and her ugly behavior, the lover's values are shaken and his world inverted. As a result, paradox often abounds. Aside from bemoaning this state of affairs, there is little that he can do, unless of course the poet is willing to extract him from the clutches of convention. This the poet is loathe to attempt. Thus, even when the speaker indulges in some wit, it is most often an ironic or paradoxical comment at his own expense. The speaker in a villanella from Giovanni da Nola's *Canzone napolitane* (second book, 1566) sets out to construct an image of his beloved that is more splendid than the sun, but after nine lines devoted to various aspects of her beauty, he concludes by endowing her with a cruel heart:

> Core crudele che mi straccia tanto
> Per che tanto crudele si ch'ogn'hora
> Dat morte a chi t'ama e chi c'adora.

(Galanti, p. 4)

Often the speaker begins by lamenting his condition (usually to Love, whose arrows have caused him anguish):

Io sto in perpetua morte, Amor crudele . . .

(Menghini, p. 444)

Tutto l'offese che m'hai fatto, amore,
Io ti perdone, poiché m'hai giurato
Di mai piú farmi stare innamorato.

(Menghini, p. 486)

M'ha punto amor con velenoso dardo . . .

(Galanti, p. 31)

Or the speaker may appeal, or complain, directly to the mistress:

Villanella crudel mi fai morire
Con la bellezza tua rara infinita.

(Galanti, p. 54)

Che sarà, donna, della vita mia?
Poiché sta mia partita
Mi dà mortal ferita.

(Menghini, p. 442)

Pietà, pietà, mercè, per Dio,
Donne leggiadre e piene di pietade . . .

(Menghini, p. 443)

In one villanella the speaker confronts Love with his problems. The beloved has become, in the inverted world of the distraught lover, the enemy:

Amor, che debbo far, che mi consigli?
La mia nemico mi s'asconde e fugge
E quanto piú la seguo piú mi strugge.

(Menghini, p. 445)

After rehearsing his dilemma, this speaker, whose approach suggests that he is attempting to deal with the situation rationally, concludes:

Cosí tra due contrarii mi consumo:
Ahi, fortuna crudel, che far mi deggio?
S'io miro ho male e s'io non miro ho peggio.

Such is the wit of the thwarted lover. A reasoned and presumably logical approach leaves him no better than he is when he yields to passionate outbursts.

These fragments offer a fair sampling of the subject matter of the sixteenth-century Italian villanella, though there is a notable number of villanelle of a more burlesque nature (Einstein, I, p. 360). It is the subject matter familiar to anyone who knows a handful of lyrics by nearly any Renaissance poet on the Continent or in England, and it may be encountered in any collection of lyric poetry written since Petrarch and continuing into the seventeenth century. One may read similar poems in English, French, Spanish, Portugese, and German. It is not, therefore, in subject or theme that the villanella may be thought of as distinctive. And, as an examination of a few of the more striking and sometimes less conventional villanelle will demonstrate, the practitioners of the form did not expand the metaphoric idiom of the day except on rare occasion, even though they had recourse, presumably, to a folk tradition.

Among the poems in Menghini's collection are several villanelle which exemplify the Renaissance taste for conceit. In the following instance the poet traces the lover's tears as they are congealed (conventionally enough) in the icy breast of his mistress, after which they become a mirror ironically reflecting his own grief.

> Le lacrime c'ho sparto un tempo, ahi lasso,
> Madonna le raccolse e con diletto
> Le ripose nel suo gelato petto.
>
> E quando in duro ghiaccio fur converse,
> Per far la vita mia trist'e dolente
> Ne fecce un specchio chiaro e transparente.
>
> Nel qual poi la crudel sera e mattina
> Si specchia nel mio lume le bellezze
> De' suoi begl'occhi e delle bionde trezze.
>
> Cosí, donne mie care e lieti amanti,
> Io so chiamato specchio di dolore,
> Dove si vede l'impietà d'Amore.

(Menghini, p. 448)

Aside from the metrical form there is nothing to identify this poem as a villanella. The icy breast and blonde tresses of the mistress are part of the stock imagery of Petrarchan convention. The setting and the personae are not of the village or country, and the poem shows no trace of Neapolitan dialect or of colloquial idiom.

The following poem from Obertello's collection, however, has certain elements that identify it as a villanella in content as well as in form. The hard-luck lover, though his condition as indicated in the refrain is conventional enough, expresses his plight in language which alludes, probably, to village life.

> Mai posso far collata che non piova;
> Tristo me ch'haggio la mall'avventura,
>   Né mal né bene longo tempo dura!
>
> Sentite tutti st'altra buona nuova:
> Mai non impegn 'e sempre pago usura,
>   Né mal né bene longo tempo dura!
>
> Metto sotto la vicola trent'ova:
> Vienne la gatta et tutti me li fura,
>   Né mal né bene longo tempo dura!
>
> Vado per comperar grano al mercato,
> Et gli dinari mi cascan del lato!
>   Et cosí acasca a chi è sventurato.

(Obertello, pp. 141–2)

In form, this is one of the least complex of the villanelle, requiring slight rhyme variation and utilizing a refrain line, which minimizes the difficulties of the *rima baciata* scheme. Its particular appeal is the poet's use of naturalistic, nonconventional imagery and his non-Petrarchan setting and perspective. In fact, the poem is not even addressed specifically to the subject of love or the beautiful mistress, and in this respect it provides a refreshing change of pace from most villanelle of the era. Is a villanella like this one popular, because it does not follow the conventional Petrarchan mode and because it does seem (in content and theme) to be closer to a folk source? I am inclined to argue that this poem is actually no more popular than the many villanelle that follow conventional lines, and I believe that a good case could be made for this poem as a product of a sophisticated poet with a stronger commitment to the villanella than most other poets of his time. (Consider, for example, the merely passing reference to the "villanella" in "Tutti amano le donne.")

Other villanelle seem popular because of their very simplicity. This is so of the following poem which, as Obertello notes, is similar to a villanella from Giovanni Nasco's *Le Canzon villanesche alla napolitana* (1565).

Quando voleva già tu non volevi,
Et or che tu voresti non vogl'io.

Io voleva, nè no, tu non volesti;
Or no vogl'io, et tu et tu voresti.

Quando chiamava et tu non respondeva;
Mi chiami hor tu, né vo risponder io.

(Obertello, p. 137)

This poem, with its simplified form and wordplay and with its lack of conventional Petrarchan usage, might be contrasted with the following more elaborate effort.

Son mort'et moro et pur cerco morire,
Né per stato morir perdo la vita.
O potentenza d'amor sol infinita!

Et bench'io moro non more il martire,
Anzi fra ghiaccio e foco ho morte e vita,
O potentenza d'amor sol infinita!

Dunque la vita mia si può ben dire
Peggio che morte chi la tienne in vita.
O potentenza d'amor sol infinita!

Questa è la vita di chi segue amore
Tra ghiaccio e foco, fra speme e timore;
Vivo morendo et no vive ne muore.

(Obertello, p. 142)

Here the poet does not simply toy with the frustrating irony of conflicting moods, but he plays on the Petrarchan concept of martyrdom to love. Both poems rely heavily on wordplay through shifting verb forms, but the second also works with balanced pairs (ghiaccio e foco, morte e vita, speme e timore) and through these, with the conventional Petrarchan antitheses that make up the paradoxical dilemma of the lover. The refrain in this poem and the regularity of form also suggest the craftsmanship of a more sophisticated poet.

One other example of a presumably popular villanella is that of Mazzone Marc'Antonio, published in Augustin Corona's *Delle Napolitane* (1570). The use of Neapolitan dialect would perhaps be sufficient for Monti to identify this poem as popular, but equally important, I think, is the scarcity of conventional Petrarchan imagery and thematic development. By now it should be clear that a more important issue than the relative popular or courtly identity of the poems is the degree to which the poet moves to sources other than Petrarch. By the mid-sixteenth century, in other words, one may presume that Petrarchism, though perhaps a necessity for most courtly poets, was accessible to whatever audience there might have been for street poetry or for other popular types. What distinguishes the various villanelle, therefore, is the extent to which the poet absorbs supposed folk elements (images, settings, characters, subjects) in his poems and the extent to which the poet departs from Petrarchism. The writer of "Mai posso far collata," therefore, writes a distinctive poem because he avoids Petrarchan convention and because he avails himself of a folk (or popular, if one prefers that designation) context. The same applies to Marc'Antonio's poem below. (Metrically, the movement from seven-syllable to eleven-syllable lines is common in the villanella.)

> Con quessa belta mano
>   Tu ti nascond'in vano
>   Ssa bella facci'altiera
>   D'innamorar ogni selvaggia fera.
>
> Quando per strada passi
>   Quessi begl'occhi abbassi
>   Che pono consolare
>   Li grandi affanni e le mie pen'amare.
>
> Com'a no cappuccino
>   Vai con lo viso chino
>   Et hai gran torto affene
>   Nasconder a chi t'ama tanto bene.
>
> Alza ss'occhi splendenti
>   Ch'allegrano le genti
>   E col tuo dolce riso
>   Consola ogn'un che mira il tuo bel viso.

> (Galanti, p. 5)

The donna is hard to get, but she is not "crudelle." The lover suffers the pangs of "amore," but not to the point of death, figuratively or otherwise. The poem is simply a complaint over the woman's modesty and an appeal to her to raise her bright eyes and to smile on her admirers. The woman in this poem exemplifies coyness rather than coquetry.

By way of contrast, consider the following villanella from Nola's

Canzon napolitane, also a poem of compliment to the donna, but conventional throughout in its language and especially conventional in its conclusion.

> Faccia mia bella piu che'l sol splendente
> Adornata d'honest'e vaghe chiome
> Che splendete'l sol con vostro chiaro lume.
>
> Viso giocondo altiero, honesto e bello
> Accompagnato dal suave riso
> Che chi ti mira mostri il paradiso.
>
> Mano molese e bianca piu che neve
> Petto dove il mio cor sempre se anida
> Geme e si lamenta e mai s'adira.
>
> Core crudele che mi straccia tanto
> Per che tanto crudele si ch'ogn'hora
> Dai morte a chi t'ama e chi t'adora.

(Galanti, p. 4)

While the imagery in neither of these poems connects them with the village, village life, or the village maiden, the perspective of the persona, the presumed male speaker in the poem, provides some clue to their disparity. One speaker is the sort who is content to say that the woman's hand is pretty. She hides herself "in vain," presumably because her hand gives evidence of her beauty. The speaker in the second poem, however, feels compelled to rhapsodize, and the source of his rhapsody is the rhetorical pool of clichéd metaphors: her soft hand is whiter than the snow. When he describes his beloved, he falls into conventional language, and this leads us to identify the poem with the courtly villanella. Whether we are justified in doing so is debatable, but certainly if the criteria used by Romeralo in his study of the villancico have any validity, the former poem is more nearly popular than the latter. Consider, for example, the use of descriptive adjectives in these poems. In the former there are eleven in sixteen lines (bella, bella, altiera, selvaggia, begli, grandi, chino, gran, splendenti, dolce, bel). These adjectives are distinctive in two ways: first, they are very simple, and second, they are redundant, with the adjectival form for beauty appropriately dominant. In the latter poem there are twelve such adjectives in twelve lines (bella, honeste, vaghe, chiaro, giocondo, altiero, honesto, bello, suave, molese, bianca, crudele). Although two of these are repeated, this list indicates considerably greater variety than the former. Even more important, however, is the poet's tendency to cluster or pair his adjectives in the poem. The adjectives are used here, as in many other sophisticated villanelle, to provide balance. They may be said to be more "rhetorical" in nature than those in the former poem. (The same may also be said for this poet's manipulation of verbs in lines 1 and 3, 9, and 12.)

It is perhaps impossible to ascertain whether Marc'Antonio's villanella was genuinely popular in its day, or whether the anonymous villanella with which I have compared it was in any sense "of the court." Certainly the latter is the more artful poem. Sophistication of artifice, however, is an elusive subject. Monti refers to "spontaneity" in opposition to artifice (pp. 220–25), but the nature of spontaneity — what qualities a spontaneously written poem possesses — he does not say. Moreover, he concludes that in some poems "elementi popolari son commisti ad elementi artificiosi" (p. 231). At one extreme of artifice, however, we might place such poems as the one below, in which the poet has contrived an elaborate metaphor drawn from chess.

> Scacchiero è diventato lo mio coro
> di turchino e di bianco e nello gioco
> la Dama con il Re son fiamma e fuoco.
>
> Li Rocchi son li miei salvi pensieri
> e le speranze mie son li Delfini,
> che per traverso vanno, li meschini!
>
> Sdegno e sospetto son li Cavalli
> che per traverso saltano nel sore
> e le Pedine son pianti e dolore.
>
> Amor gioca con me e va cercando,
> se non m'aiuta tua beltà divina,
> di darmi scacco matto di pedina.

(Monti, p. 247)

It is evident enough that this poem was created by a cultivated poet for a courtly audience, certainly not "spontaneously." It may reasonably be argued, however, that a poem in which the imagery and circumstances are drawn from the village fountain and marketplace was not written by or for villagers, but by a sophisticated poet for a courtly audience that could be charmed by a poem about a village maiden as easily as it could by one about a shepherdess or about the chess game of love.

What sustained the villanella, however, was not the achievement of any poet, known or anonymous, writing folk, popular, semipopular, spontaneous, sophisticated, artificial, or courtly versions. Nor was it the appeal of the form itself, either as quatrains composed in *rima baciata*, or as tercets. The fact that a considerable variety of poets was, apparently, writing villanelle does give the form some latitude in subject matter, theme, and texture (diction, imagery, figurative language). It was the use of the villanella in part-singing and chamber music, however, that established its vogue not only in Italy, but also throughout Europe by the latter half of the sixteenth century.[16] Although I am concerned primarily with the characteristics of the Italian villanella as poetry, it is important that something be said of its development in the vocal music of the era.

Everett Helm dates the revival of Italian music from 1480 and associates it with the Florentine carnival song and the Mantuan frottola, both forms, it should be noted, connected with northern Italy.[17] It is the frottola, as Alfred Einstein observes, that is the embryonic stage of both the madrigal and the villanella.[18] Some musicologists have argued that the frottola has antecedents in popular dance-song, but Helm notes that it was "cultivated mainly for or by the nobility" and that Pietro Bembo was influential in its development, thus suggesting that "the poetry was anything but popular, despite occasional folklike reminiscences in certain pieces" (p. 394). The problems of popular poetry apply somewhat to the music of the villanella (as to the frottola before it), as we shall see. That the music is composed by sophisticated, courtly musicians, however, is indisputable. Helm describes the frottola music as "nonexpressive — often pleasant, sometimes gauche, but never passionate"; unsentimental in content, "the frottola is pointed, often epigrammatic, frivolous, banal" (p. 397). In the context of the frottola, Helm examines the "pseudopopular *strambotto*" (p. 391), which was included in collections of frottole. The strambotto originated in Sicily as early as the late fourteenth century. Its reappearance, notably in Ottaviano dei Petrucci's fourth frottola collection (1505), is indicative of the growing interest in Italian folk or popular music in courtly circles.

The four-part harmonic structure, according to Helm, is its "most immediately striking feature" (p. 400). The structure is "essentially homophonic," but imitative counterpoint, anticipating madrigal structure, develops in later settings. Rhythmic definiteness and harmonic precision are two traits of the frottola which, according to Einstein, identify the form with an attempt to achieve a popular manner. Clearly the villanella as we have encountered it after 1537 is several removes from any genuinely popular or folk origins. As the frivolity of the frottola gave way to sentimentality and epigrammatic point, the madrigal developed; as the frivolity became more pronounced, the villanella and related forms (e.g., *villotta*, *mascherata*) developed (Einstein, p. 107). The term "madrigal," which was applied to a fourteenth-century form, first appears in its polyphonic, sixteenth-century character in the *Madrigali de diversi musici libro primo* of 1530. The term "villanella," as applied to the musical form rather than simply to the village maiden, appears first in the *Canzone villanesche alla napolitana* in 1537. By 1568 the term "villanella" had largely replaced "villanesche" and "napolitana" (or was used in combination), so that Nola's *Canzone villanesche* (1541, 1545) is titled *Villanelle alla napolitana* after 1567. Although the villanelle and other light modes of the sixteenth century stand in "emphatic opposition" to the more serious and more highly "literary" madrigal, Einstein stresses that they were not genuinely popular, but were composed for the same audience (p. 340).

The villanella, in fact, often parodies or burlesques the madrigal. "The villanella," writes E. J. Dent, "is generally in three parts and homophonic; its main characteristic is plentiful use of consecutive triads." The most striking feature of its structure is the "unorthodox harmony in consecutive fifths," a practice prohibited by conventional theory of the age.[19] Since intervals of thirds and fifths are the easiest to sing (easiest to keep in tune, and especially for one with an untutored voice), it may be deduced that the prohibition of fifths was a part of the commitment to virtuosity and high artifice meant to sustain the distance between courtly and popular music. The madrigal is generally in four or more parts and polyphonic (though imitative counterpoint often alternates with homophonic sections). Harmonic coloring or word-painting is common, especially in the later madrigals of such masters as Luca Marenzio (1553–99). This practice is contradicted, of course, by the plainness of the villanella, and perhaps is ridiculed by the use of fifths to create an impression of rusticity. The villanella retains the simplicity and liveliness (generally without sentimentality) necessitated by its use as dance music, and scholars have found evidence of its use for serenades, sometimes with instrumental accompaniment.[20] In the hands of later composers, like Marenzio, however, the villanella loses much of its contrived rusticity and is often set to four or more voices.

In order to get a clearer since of the villanella as music it is necessary to examine a representative score. In this undertaking, however, I do not intend to do more than touch upon some fairly obvious elements of the musical form, and I do not pretend any special competence in the area of music theory or composition. The early masters of the villanella (often composers of the madrigal as well) include Nola, Tomaso Cimello, Perissone Cambio, Giovan Tommasso di Maio, and Adrian Willaert. Nola, Maio, and Cimello were Neapolitans, and the anonymous collection of 1537 was printed in Naples, but subsequent collections (beginning in 1541) were printed in Venice, the center of sixteenth-century Italian music, and most of the other composers were not Neapolitans. Maio (ca. 1490–1550), considered by Einstein to be perhaps the "oldest and earliest master" of the villanella (I, p. 353), sets a poem which is representative of the low comic or burlesque aspects of the form.

> Tutte le vecchie son maleciose
> C'hanno perduta la stascione vera
> Questo lo dico a te vecchia tramera.
>
> Superb' ingrate: misere: e letrose
> Chinollo crede: mir al'ala cera
> Questo lo dico a te vecchia tramera.
>
> La meglio parte: so tutte picose
> Che fanno se non tossero la sera
> Questo lo dico a te vecchia tramera.
>
> Fuggite tutte ste vecchiarde amare
> Citelle che c'havite ammaritare
> Stat'a piacer' fatele crepare.

(Einstein, III, pp. xviii–xix)

Since the villanella usually consists of four stanzas, only the first stanza (in this, as in many cases, just three lines) is set. Since the madrigal is essentially just a single stanza (usually eight or ten lines), the entire poem is set. The setting of this villanella (Einstein, III, p. 79) may be reproduced, since only three lines of poetry are involved, in a relatively small space.

Tutte le vecchie

Tut- te le vec- chie tut- te le vec- chie son ma- le- ci-
-o- se C'han- no per- du- ta la sta-scio- ne ve-
-ra c'han- no per- du- ta la sta-scio- ne ve- ra Que- sto lo
di-co a te que- sto lo di-co a te vec- chia tra-me- ra. Que- ra.

What should be noticed most readily in this composition is its simple,
homophonic structure and its plain, uncomplicated rhythm. The fourth
and fifth measures provide the most striking example of the use of parallel or consecutive fifths, but fifths also appear in the tenth and fourteenth measures and are thus established as a significant feature of the
score.

The simplicity of this piece may be best appreciated by contrast
with the polyphonic texture of the madrigal. Since the settings for most
madrigals are considerably longer than those for villanelle, I offer the
opening 10½ measures of Marenzio's setting for "Scaldava il sol," from
a poem by Luigi Alamanni (1495–1556), born in Florence but an exile
at the court in Paris most of his life.

Scaldavail sol

Whereas the three voices singing the simple, homophonic villanella merely repeat certain phrases of the poem in unison, the five voices of the polyphonic madrigal play extensively with the phrases so that a single phrase of 1½ measures ("scaldava il sol") actually extends over five measures in Marenzio's setting. Moreover, as the phrase is repeated certain key words or syllables (*sol*, gior*no*, ar*co*) are emphasized by use of half or whole notes against the rush of quarters and eighths (especially at the end of the section, in which "l'arco," the last word of the opening line of the poem, is repeated). Marenzio's selection of a text by a known poet suggests the madrigal writers' preference for serious poetry of some literary quality rather than anonymous *poesia per musica*, which predominates in villanella collections.

The later masters of the villanella, the most noteworthy being Marenzio himself, include Giovanni Nasco (d. 1561), Orlando di Lasso (ca. 1532–94), Giaches de Wert (1536–96), Baldisserra Donato (d. 1603), and such noted German composers as Jakob Regnart (d. 1600, a Netherlander employed in German courts) and Johann Nauwach (fl. 1620–40). Lasso's edition, published in Antwerp in 1555, had conveyed the villanella across the Alps, although it had been transmitted widely in Venetian printings after 1537. Between 1567 and 1584, the date of Marenzio's first book of villanelle, Monti counts some one hundred new and reprinted collections of villanelle; he notes that the last published collection of villanelle appeared in 1631 (p. 14). Einstein observes that toward the end of the sixteenth century the villanella "becomes respectable" (I, p. 383), inclining toward the madrigal in a spirit of dependence rather than parody.

In Italian poetry it cannot be said that the villanella achieves much stature. It seems always to have been regarded as poetry in the service of the musician, and the musicians do not seem to have had the same respect for the poetic texts of the villanelle that they did for those of the madrigals. Moreover, like most Italian poetry of the era, the villanella reflects the desire of well-meaning but reactionary humanists, like Bembo, to recapture the greatness of the fourteenth century, of Petrarch. The occasional popular or folk strain, sometimes of the coarse or burlesque sort that relates the villanella to the *mascherata* and the *moresca*, at least in spirit, appears to be some distance from whatever folk origins there might have been.[22] It is best then to consider the Italian villanella of the sixteenth century not semipopular, but quasipopular, the product, for the most part, of conscious imitation of a popular source. When the enthusiams of the composers (and of the courts) waned in favor of the canzonetta, the villanella was without a future in Italian literature.

◆

2.
The Villanelle in
Sixteenth-Century French Poetry

Gennaro Maria Monti writes that by the latter half of the sixteenth century the villanella was being composed in the most diverse stanzaic forms, with varied line lengths and rhyme schemes: "Le villanelle dell'ultimo periodo, variate in tutti i possibili modi, con i versi più varie, rappresentano l'ultima evoluzione del genere; il Chiabrera e il Rinuccini imitando — dalle poesie di Ronsard e della *Plejade* o da altre forme popolari e dotte italiane — l'uso delle rime alternate e incrociate, diedero nuova vita alle villanelle trasformate."[1] Curiously enough, the apparent dissolution of the form after the middle of the century, both in Italy and in France, where it was a newcomer, was to end just as the century lapsed. French poets of the sixteenth century, some of them well-known members of the Pléiade, moved toward defining or fixing the form, generally on a stanza of four to eight lines, including a one- or two-line refrain, and with slight rhyme variation. The fixed form devised by Jean Passerat, however, was not to have an immediate impact, even on those poets of the early seventeenth century who remained sympathetic to the forms and themes of the Pléiade.

Exactly when or how the villanelle came into French poetry is not certain. Warner Forrest Patterson's study of French prosody identifies Melin de Saint-Gelais' "Villanesque," published in 1547 but probably composed earlier, as the first poem of the type in French. Saint-Gelais (1487–1558) spent some time at Padua, and if his poem were closer to the Italian villanelle being composed at the time, one might be inclined to argue for a direct line of influence. As it stands, there are several points of possible connection with the Italian villanella, the most obvious, perhaps, being the couplet (*rima baciata*) scheme, here set up as six-line stanzas.

> Je ne say que c'est qu'il me faut
> Froid ou chaud;
> Je ne dors plus ny je ne veille,
> C'est merveille
> De me voir sain et langoureux;
> Je croy que je suis amoureux.
> En quatre jours je ne fais pas
> Deux repas,
> Je ne voy ne beufs ne charrue;
> J'ay la rue
> Pour me promener nuict et jour,
> Et fuy l'hostel et le sé jour.

The play with line length is not common to the Italian villanella, nor is it a feature of most later French villanelles. Of course the theme of the poem is familiar enough—the conflicts which beset the rejected lover—and there are some other characteristics common to the Italian villanella. At the dance, for instance, there are crude references to the village girl.

> Je ne say où mal me tient,
> Mais il vient
> D'avoir dansé avec Catin.
> Son tetin
> Alloit au bransle, et maudit sois-je,
> Il estoit aussi blanc que neige.

The green-eyed village girl eyes him askance, but when he pursues her she turns her back on him. He concludes:

> Si ceste contenance fiere
> Dure guere,
> Á dieu grange, à dieu labourage!
> J'ay courage
> De ne voir gendarme un matin,
> Ou moyne, en despit de Catin.[2]

Here and elsewhere in the poem, for example, when the villager blushes and must hide behind his handkerchief, Saint-Gelais sustains the context of the village flirtation, and in this respect the sophisticated French poets are often even more true to the nature of the genre than many of the anonymous Italian poets.

Although Ronsard apparently wrote no villanelles, most of the other Pléiade poets and some of their successors did. Joachim du Bellay's "J'ai trop servi," which Patterson labels a "villanesque," is clearly modelled on the Italian tercet villanella. In 1553 Du Bellay, then about 31, accompanied his cousin, Cardinal Jean du Bellay, on a mission to Rome, where he stayed for about four years. His exposure to the popular Italian form may well have come from that sojourn, and his best known villanelle, "En ce moys délicieux," in *Divers jeux rustiques* (1558), which was influenced by the Latin poems of Naugerius (Navagero), is definitely a product of his stay in Rome.

Many of the sixteenth-century French villanelles, like Saint-Gelais' 54-line "Villanesque" just examined, are more elaborate than most of the Italian villanelle, but Du Bellay's Italianate villanelle fits the type which Monti classifies as IVe (*ab*B), even to the hendecasyllabic line.

> J'ay trop servi de fable au populaire
> En vous aymant, trop ingrate maistresse:
> Suffise vous d'avoir eu ma jeunesse.
>
> J'ay trop cherché les moyens de complaire
> A vos beau yeux, causes de ma detresse:
> Suffise vous d'avoir eu ma jeunesse.
>
> Il vous falloit me tromper ou m'attraire
> Dedans vos lacs d'une plus fine addresse:
> Suffise vous d'avoir eu ma jeunesse.
>
> Car la raison commence à se distraire
> Du fol amour qui trop cruel m'oppresse:
> Suffise vous d'avoir eu ma jeunesse.[3]

As in many of the Italian villanelle, the distressed lover addresses an ungrateful mistress who has sapped him of his youth. This particular villanelle is not of interest except as an example of the direct relationship between the French villanelle and the Italian villanella in the century.

Du Bellay's villanelle, "A vous, troppe legere," in which the giddy wind acquires feminine qualities, is written from the perspective of a wheat harvester who offers flowers and whose labor is eased by the wind's sweet breath.

> De vostre douce haleine
> Eventez ceste plaine,
> Eventez ce sejour,
> Cependant que j'ahanne
> A mon blé, que se vanne
> A la chaleur du jour.[4]

More typical of the villanelle, at least in its Italian form, is "En ce moys délicieux," in which the male speaker laments the contrast between the fair weather outside and the personal misery which is caused by "Belle et franche Marguerite."

En ce moys délicieux,
Qu'amour toute chose incite,
Un chacun à qui mieulx mieulx
La doulceur du temps imite,
Mais une rigeur despite
Me faict pleurer mon malheur.
Belle et franche Marguerite,
Pour vous j'ay ceste douleur.

Dedans vostre oeil gracieux
Toute doulceur est escritte,
Mais la doulceur de voz yeulx
En amertume est confite.
Souvent la couleuvre habite
Dessoubs une belle fleur.
Belle et franche Marguerite,
Pour vous j'ay ceste douleur.

Or puis que je deviens vieux,
Et que rien ne me profite,
Désespéré d'avoir mieulx,
Je m'en iray rendre hermite,
Je m'en iray rendre hermite,
Pour mieulx pleurer mon malheur.
Belle et franche Marguerite,
Pour vous j'ay ceste douleur.

Mais si la faveur des Dieux
Au bois vous avoit conduitte,
Où, despéré d'avoir mieulx,
Je m'en iray rendre hermite,
Peult estre que ma poursuite
Vous feroit changer couleur.
Belle et franche Marguerite,
Pour vous j'ay ceste douleur.

(Du Bellay, pp. 27–28)

Although the form of the poem is not similar to any of those generally used in the Italian villanelle, the use of refrain and the frequent repetition of key words and lines are in keeping with the tendency of the villanelle to indulge in recurrence, an essential trait of the form as eventually defined by Passerat. Twice the assonance or internal rhyme —

pleurer, malheur, douleur—joins in a sort of triumvirate of misery, and the same vowel sound also figures in other combinations, for example, in the contrast of *douleur* with *doulceur*. In the last two stanzas (aside from the refrain) key lines or phrases are repeated five times, the most obvious, and therefore most emphatic, instance being the three appearances of the line, "Je m'en iray rendre hermite."

A 36-line villanelle in quatrains by the minor Pléiade poet, Étienne Jodelle (1532–1573), anticipates Passerat's form more nearly than any prior effort by a French poet, including even Du Bellay's villanelle in tercets.

Cent foys j'ay tasché me distraire,
Des feux d'un amoureux pensers
Mais je n'ay peu tant avancer
Car le destin m'est adversaire.

C'est un mal qui m'est ordinaire
D'aymer ce que j'avoy domté
Je sçay bien sa legereté
Mais quoy? le destin m'est contraire.

C'est bien le Ciel qui peust substraire
Mon coeur, ma flame et mon devoir
Ce que je veux est sans pouvoir
Car j'ay le Destin adversaire.

Rien que mon mal ne me peust plaire
C'est bien mon mal que de l'aymer
Semblable aux vagues de la mer
Mais quoy! le destin m'est contraire.

J'ay beau mile sermens me faire
Puis qu'un seul trait d'affexion
Guaigne ma resolution
Car j'ay le Destin adversaire.

L'amour n'est rien qu'une misere
Ostant les yeux, la liberté
Ostant mesme la volonté
Lors qu'on a le destin contraire.

Seul destin qui fait me desplaire
Ce que de deusse plus aymer
N'aymant rien qu'à me consumer
Au feu d'un destin adversaire.

Telle qu'une onde passagere
Qui trainne une moisson de fleurs

Je vois enlever mes ardeurs
Aux flos de mon destin contraire.

C'est pourquoy je me désespere
Ne pouvant rien sur mon vouloir
Esclave d'un autre pouvoir
Quand le destin m'est adversaire.[5]

Like Passerat's villanelle, Jodelle's is limited to two rhymes recurring in an enclosed (*rima incrociate*) pattern (*abba*). Moreover, with some variations, the refrain lines alternate, the *adversaire* with the *contraire*, similar to the way the refrain lines work in Passerat's poem. In fact, as we will see later, the variations on the refrain anticipate those employed by many twentieth-century American writers of the villanelle.

There is scant evidence in Jodelle's poem of any interest in the village or rural life or setting, and although the speaker is a conventional despairing lover, the repetition of *destin* throughout, with some play on its connotation, lends a peculiar seriousness to this villanelle. The concepts of contrariety and adversity are played upon variously in the poem, though here they are not related to the perverse mistress, as is most often the case, but to love itself, or perhaps to some force even more distant which dominates the speaker. The *mal* of the first line of the second stanza, for example, is played against the *bien* of the first line of the third stanza. In the fourth stanza, "C'est bien mon mal," the two come together paradoxically. Similarly, the fires and flame of the hapless love are related to the fire of an adverse destiny in the seventh stanza, and then to a passing wave and to the floodtide of contrary destiny in the eighth. Verbs indicating power or mastery in the poem (*domté, pouvoir, peust, guaigne,* et al.) are played against those suggesting surrender or flight (*me distraire, substraire, ostant, me consumer,* et al.) At last, unable to satisfy his wishes and deprived of both liberty and will, the speaker becomes slave to another power, a destiny, in fact, which appears to have surpassed in might the fickleness of any woman. The inescapability of his predicament has in fact been apparent from the first stanzas. He can make no progress because destiny is his adversary; and, even though he understands the inconsistencies of love, he cannot avoid them since his destiny is so contrary as to compel him to be in love.

Philippe Desportes, about twelve years Passerat's junior, may well have written his two villanelles after Passerat's, but there is no evidence that Passerat's poems were published before 1597, and the date of their composition is unknown. Since Passerat wrote a sonnet in response to one in Desportes' *Diane* (1573), there is no doubt that the men knew each other's work, and Passerat's fixed-form model might well have circulated in manuscript. If Desportes did know "J'ai perdu ma tourterelle" and Passerat's new villanelle form, his poems show no evidence that he was influenced by it. His poems are more reminiscent in both form and content of Du Bellay's "En ce moys délicieux," which had been published in 1558. In both poems the speaker is a steadfast male protesting the inconstancy of his mistress. "M'ostant le fruit de ma fidelle attente" consists of six sestets (*ababcC*), similar in rhyme pattern to the *ottava rima*. The speaker protests his faithfulness and inveighs against the deceit to which he is so susceptible.

> M'ostant le fruit de ma fidelle attente,
> On veut, helas! que je sois un rocher,
> Que je me taise et que rien je ne sente;
> Mais si grand dueil, que je ne puis cacher,
> Fend ma poitrine et fait que je m'escrie:
> Il est aisé de tromper qui se fie![6]

The "fruit" of his service has been ill treatment at the hands of the fickle mistress, so in the fourth stanza he warns: "Jamais ton nom en mes vers ne se lise." The poem concludes with a warning to the happy lover who is now tasting the sweet fruits of the former lover's still unnamed mistress: "A tels appas elle arresta ma vie;/J'en fus trompé, jamais je ne m'y fie."

"Rozette, pour un peu d'absence" is quite similar in form to Du Bellay's "En ce moys délicieux" (Desportes' rhyme scheme is *ababcdCD*, Du Bellay's is *ababbcBC*). Unlike Du Bellay, Desportes varies the first refrain line throughout the poem. Desportes' Rozette, unlike Du Bellay's Marguerite, is designated a shepherdess, but aside from that he makes little effort to sustain the atmosphere of village or countryside.

> Rozette, pour un peu d'absence,
> Vostre coeur vous avez changé,
> Et moy, sçachant cette inconstance,
> Le mien autre part j'ay rangé;
> Jamais plus beauté si legere
> Sur moy tant de pouvoir n'aura:
> Nous verrons, volage bergere,
> Qui premier s'en repentira.
>
> Tandis qu'en pleurs je me consume,
> Maudissant cet esloignement,
> Vous, qui n'aimez que par coustume,

Caressiez un nouvel amant.
Jamais legere girouette
Au vent si tost ne se vira;
Nous verrons, bergere Rozette,
Qui premier s'en repentira.

Où sont tant de promesses saintes,
Tant de pleurs versez en partant?
Est-il vray que ces tristes plaintes
Sortissent d'un coeur inconstant?
Dieux, que vous estes mensongere!
Maudit soit qui plus vous croira!
Nous verrons, volage bergere,
Qui premier s'en repentira.

Celuy qui a gaigné ma place,
Ne vous peut aimer tant que moy;
Et celle que j'aime vous passe
De beauté, d'amour et de foy.
Gardez bien vostre amitié neuve,
La mienne plus ne varira,
Et puis nous verrons à l'espreuve
Qui premier s'en repentira.

(Desportes, pp. 450–51)

The theme of this poem is essentially the same as that of "M'ostant le fruit," but the speaker, notably in the third stanza, appears to be more outraged and more passionate than the speaker in Desportes' other villanelle. Moreover, the speaker concludes by posing the prospect of another woman, thus making good on the implied threat of the refrain.

Probably the least prominent among the writers of the villanelle in sixteenth-century France is Jean Palerne (1557– 1592?), whose *Peregrinations*, recounting a tour of the Mediterranean islands, North Africa, and the Near East, was published in 1606. In form Palerne's villanelle (*aab*CCB) is reminiscent of some Italian villanelle, and the manuscript version includes two Italian poems, one of four couplets and the other in tercets. Although the mistress is praised throughout the first half of the poem, it is apparent from the refrain that the lover's success with her is not assured.

Le feu secret de mon désir
M'a faict une dame choisir,
    Belle par excellence.
    Un amoureulx
    Est malheureulx
    Oui n'a la joyssance.

The theme, however, does differ from most of those played upon in French villanelles of the age. The poem ends with an appeal to the mistress rather than a complaint over her inconstancy.

> Dame, que je sers humblement,
> Donnez-moy donc présentement
>   Le doux bien que je pense.
>   Un amoureulx
>   Est malheureulx
>   Qui n'a la joyssance.[7]

Of all the sixteenth-century French poets who attempted the villanelle, however, the most important is Jean Passerat (1534– 1602), best known in his lifetime as a scholar. Born at Troyes, he held a chair in humanities at Paris, first at the *collège du Plessis* and then at the *collège du Cardinal-Lemoine*. After studying the law for two or three years at Bourges with the renowned Cujas, Passerat traveled through Italy, returning to Paris in 1569. When Peter Ramus was killed during the St. Bartholomew's Day massacre of 1572, Passerat replaced him in the chair of eloquence and Latin poetry at Paris. The Catholic League's agitations caused the temporary suspension of his work, but he returned to his chair with Henry IV's entrance into Paris in 1594. His best known literary achievement is his contribution to the *Satire Menipée* (1594). Pierre Blanchemain, his modern editor, finds in Passerat's poetry a certain frigidity and only rare moments of "le cri véritable de la passion"; moreover, "Ce n'est certes pas dans les vers de commande que Passerat excelle, mais dans la fine raillerie."[8] Blanchemain, however, finds the villanelle, "J'ai perdu ma tourterelle," to represent "un sentiment aimable."

Passerat's villanelle, "Qui en sa fantasie," is close to the Italian villanella type A[1] defined by Monti.[9] The form is a quatrain composed of two short-lined couplets (*rima baciata*), the latter couplet serving as a refrain throughout.

> Qui en sa fantasie
> Loge la jalousie,
> Bien tost cocu sera
> Et ne s'en sauvera.
>
> Qu'on mette une cage
> C'est oiseau sans plumage.
> Bien tost cocu sera,
> Et ne s'en sauvera.
>
> A contempler sa mine,

Qu'une coesse embeguine,
Bien tost cocu sera,
Et ne s'en sauvera.

Son front, qui bien retire
A un cornu Satyre,
Bien tost cornu sera
Et ne s'en sauvera.

(Passerat, Bk. I, pp. 165–66)

This villanelle, which is obviously not in the form that became the paradigm for later villanelles, is also similar to the Italian villanelle which pertain to coarse subjects (note the jocular variation in the refrain in the last stanza) and which appear, at least in contents, to be of popular origin.

I cite the above villanelle primarily as evidence of Passerat's probable familiarity with the Italian villanella tradition. Warner Patterson argues that the French villanelle "is an offshoot of an irregular type of virelai" such as Eustache Deschamps' "Sui je, sui je, sui je belle."[10] The idea of alternating refrain lines, however, could as easily have come from Du Bellay's villanelle quoted earlier. The now familiar model for subsequent villanelles combines the Italian tercet form, with its limited rhymes, persistent refrain, and brevity, with the virelai, perhaps from Deschamps via Du Bellay, with its alternating refrain lines and equally limited rhymes.

J'ay perdu ma Tourterelle:
Est-ce point celle que j'oy?
Je veus aller aprés elle.

Tu regretes ta femelle,
Helas! aussi fai-je moy,
J'ay perdu ma Tourterelle.

Si ton Amour est fidelle,
Aussi est ferme ma foy,
Je veus aller aprés elle.

Ta plainte se renouvelle;
Tousiours plaindre je me doy.
J'ay perdu ma Tourterelle.

En ne voyant plus la belle
Plus rien de beau je ne voy:
Je veus aller aprés elle.

Mort, que tant de fois j'appelle,
Pren ce qui se donne à toy:
J'ay perdu ma Tourterelle,
Je veus aller aprés elle.

(Passerat, Bk. II, p. 83)

Perhaps the most intriguing thing about this poem is that despite the interest among Passerat's contemporaries in the villanelle and the general inclination of the Pléiade poets and their followers to embrace fixed forms, this villanelle attracted no imitators for nearly three hundred years.

The colloquy of a forlorn lover with a turtledove (or some other appropriate bird) is hardly an innovation, though its introduction into the villanelle does appear to have been singular. It brings into the conventional setting an almost *précieuse* sort of affectation and prettiness, in some ways anticipating the mode of the next century. Much of the appeal of this poem results from the form itself, but there is also something to be said for the rather simple statement which, particularly in the last stanza, achieves a sort of poignance. The poem is quiet, the lover sad. These conditions could hardly differ more from those encountered in most Italian villanelle or other French villanelles, in which the lover is generally either outraged or torn by conflicting passions. This villanelle is almost unique in its "sympathetic" theme. Most of the villanelles we have examined may be said to thrive on paradox, contradiction, conflict, inconsistency. Palerne's "Le feu secret de mon désir" is probably the closest in sentiment to Passerat's villanelle, but its conclusion seems almost insipid beside that of Passerat. I am not trying to imply here any particular profundity for Passerat's villanelle. It is, finally, the very simplicity of statement and modulation of tone that give this poem its appeal. A literal English translation of the concluding couplet, depriving it of its lyricism, shows how plainspoken this poem really is: "I have lost my turtledove,/I want to go after her."[11]

The only French poet of any note to publish villanelles in the seventeenth century was the pastoral novelist, Honoré D'Urfé, whose lengthy masterpiece, *L'Astrée* (published between 1607 and 1628), includes several villanelles, none of which appears to owe anything to Passerat's model. D'Urfé does seems, however, to have intended to define a particular form for the villanelle. All of his villanelles follow the pattern: AAbccbAA, deedAA, fggfAA, etc. They range in length from four to six stanzas. In two instances the refrain is set apart from the body of the poem initially, so that the form is reminiscent of the Spanish villancico with its opening *estribillo*, in which the theme of the poem is announced.

The "Villanelle d'Amidor reprochant une legereté" follows an account in prose of the conventional context for the villanelle, at least as it has been reported in literature: "L'apres-dinée, nous avions accoustumé de nous assembler sous quelques arbres, et là danser aux chansons."[12]

> A la fin celuy l'aura,
> Qui dernier la servira.
> De ce coeur cent fois volage,
> Plus que le vent aimé,
>   Qui peut croire d'estre aimé,
>
> Ne doit pas estre creu sage:
> Car en fin celuy l'aura,
> Qui dernier la servira.
>
>   A tous vents la girouette,
> Sur le faiste d'une tour,
> Elle aussi vers toute amour
> Tourne le coeur et la teste:
>   A la fin celuy l'aura,
>   Qui dernier la servira.
>
>   Le chasseur jamais ne prise
> Ce qu'à la fin il a pris,
> L'inconstante fait bien pis,
> Mesprisant qui la tient prise:
>   Mais en fin celuy l'aura,
>   Qui dernier la servira.
>
>   Ainsi qu'un clou l'autre chasse
> Dedans son coeur le dernier,
> De celuy, qui fut premier,
> Soudain usurpe la place:
>   C'est pourquoy celuy l'aura,
>   Qui dernier la servira.

(D'Urfé, Vol. I, pp. 200–201)

Some of the language and imagery of this poem is reminiscent of that in Desportes' "Rozette, pour un peu d'absence." In both poems there is a fickle (*volage*) woman who is likened to a weathervane (*girouette*). Moreover, in both poems the speaker expresses a sarcastic response to female inconstancy. D'Urfé may, in fact, be playing on Desportes' refrain, "Nous verrons, volage bergere,/Qui premier s'en repentira," by offering

an antithesis (*premier–dernier*): "A la fin celuy l'aura,/Qui dernier la servira."
The concluding variations on the refrains in both poems also under-
score the similar development of the arguments.

In "Villanelle: Change d'humeur qui s'y plaira," the proud Hylas
boasts his constancy. Although the refrains in D'Urfé's other villanelles
include variations which alter their statement somewhat, the refrain in
this villanelle, like Hylas, presumably, is unchanging.

> Change d'humeur qui s'y plaira,
> Jamais Hylas ne changera.

I

> Ceux qui veulent vivre en servage,
> Peuvent comme esclaves mourir,
> Hylas jamais n'a peu souffrir
> Que l'on luy fist un tel outrage.
> Change d'humeur qui s'y plaira,
> Jamais Hylas ne changera.

II

> Il est certain, Hylas vous aime.
> Mais vous sçavez, belle Alexis,
> De son amour, quel est le prix:
> Le prix d'amour, c'est l'amour mesme.
> Change d'humeur qui s'y plaira,
> Jamais Hylas ne changera.

III

> Languir aupres d'une cruelle,
> C'est un bien maigre passe-temps,
> Et c'est en quoy je ne m'entends,
> Il vaut mieux estre infidelle.
> Change d'humeur qui s'y plaira,
> Jamais Hylas ne changera.

IV

> Mais pour ne le trouver estrange,
> Qu'égale entre nous soit la loy:
> Comme je vous ayme, aymez moy,
> Et me changez si je vous change.
> Change d'humeur qui s'y plaira,
> Jamais Hylas ne changera.

V

Ainsi d'une si douce vie
Nul de nous ne se lassera,
Parce que celuy changera
Qui premier en aura envie.
Change d'humeur qui s'y plaira,
Jamais Hylas ne changera.

VI

Et si jamais je vous en blasme,
Que je puisse mourir d'amour,
Ou bien que j'ayme quelque jour
Longuement une laide femme.
Change d'humeur qui s'y plaira,
Jamais Hylas ne changera.

(D'Urfé, Vol. III, pp. 345–46)

For Hylas, "un des chefs d'oeuvres de l'Auteur," according to Vaganay in his "Clé de *L'Astrée*," D'Urfé combined various traits of at least three French noblemen "pour en faire un inconstant, mais d'une humeur si agréable, qu'il fait toute la joye des bergers du lignon" (Vol. V, p. 549). Hylas, therefore, is the presumed antithesis, like most denizens of the villanelle, of the inconstant mistress, but in fact he is a weathervane himself. One might go so far as to argue that the ironic mode of this poem anticipates a new era in poetry which would not be interested in pastorals or ostensibly rustic Petrarchan lyrics like the villanelle.

The connections between the French villanelle and the Italian villanella are generally rather loose, but it is clear that the Italian forms did influence the French. Whether poets like Du Bellay and Passerat met the form while in Italy, or whether they encountered it via Italian songbooks in France is uncertain, but certainly the French villanelle does not start from popular origins in French poetry, or even from semi- or quasipopular origins. The villanelle was written in France by sophisticated poets who were dabbling in various forms and genres, not by anonymous poets supplying material for musical compositions, presumably from village and street. Moreover, the number of villanelles extant in sixteenth- and seventeenth-century French poetry is very slight when compared with that of the Italian villanella. It is curious, therefore, that it is the French villanelle which has survived, and that the fixed-form version of Passerat has survived the near oblivion of its singularity. The villanelle as it eventually migrated in its fixed form is also a tribute to the craftsmanship of the minor poet, for it is the villanelle contrived by Passerat that is the direct ancestor of the form as it is today, and not the inventions of his more illustrious predecessors and contemporaries.

◆

3.
The Revival of
a "Poetical Trifle"

*C*ertainly to his contemporaries the part of Jean Passerat (1534–1602) in the *Satire Ménipée* overshadowed such a trivial piece as his fixed-form villanelle, "J'ai perdu ma tourterelle." Although George Saintsbury, in his *Short History of French Literature*, refers to Passerat's villanelle as "probably the most elegant specimen of a poetical trifle that the age produced,"[1] it was just such a trifle that the next age was to reject. Yet it seems odd, despite the repudiation of the Pléiade by Malherbe and Boileau in the seventeenth century, that Passerat's invention had no immediate imitators. Certainly Passerat's reputation was secure. Ronsard himself had addressed his "L'Hylas" to Passerat in 1569.[2] Various irregular form villanelles were written by such notable figures as Desportes, Mellin de Saint-Gelays, Du Bellay, Jacques Grévin, Honoré d'Urfé, and Estienne Jodelle. Why, then, was Passerat's ultimately rather influential fixed-form villanelle not embraced, and indeed not even revived, for nearly two and a half centuries?

The answer to this question has already been given, at least in part. Neither the seventeenth century nor the eighteenth were especially hospitable to the old, overworked forms of the Renaissance. There are other reasons, though, for the snubbing of Passerat's villanelle. A review of them might provide some explanation for the curious fact that the villanelle has been considerably more important to English and American poetry than it has been to French, and that, despite the severe demands of the form on the relatively rhyme-poor English lexicon.

To begin with, the villanelle as a subgenre of lyric poetry appears to have made very little impression on the writers of prosodic texts prior to the mid-nineteenth century, when Théodore de Banville resurrected the form in his "Villanelle de Buloz," which was published in his *Odes funambulesques* (1857). Pierre de Laudun's *L'Art poétique françois* (1597) surveys a number of forms, including the madrigal, the virelay, and the triolet, but he makes no mention of the villanelle, fixed-form or otherwise. Vauquelin de la Fresnaye, however, in the Alexandrines of his *L'Art poétique françois* (1605), describes the villanelle in the general terms appropriate to the form as it was used in the music of the age:

> La chanson amoureuse affable et naturelle
> Sans sentir rien de l'Art, comme une villanelle,
> Marche parmy le peuple aux danses aux festins,
> Et raconte aux carfours les gestes des mutins.[3]

The somewhat condescending tone here, "rien de l'Art," may account for the fact that most manuals of versification during the seventeenth century do not list the villanelle at all. Neither Boileau, in *L'Art poétique* (1674), nor François Colletet, in *Le Parnasse françois* (1664), mentions the villanelle among the many forms surveyed.

The exclusion of the villanelle from prosodic texts of the age, however, was not complete. In La Sieur De la Croix's *L'Art de poésie françoise et latine* (1694), Passerat heads the list of the 67 most renowned modern poets, and his fixed-form villanelle is quoted as an example of his achievement. Moreover, De la Croix's definition of the villanelle, which he traces from the Spanish *villancico* (peasant song), is somewhat at odds with the comment of Vauquelin. It is "une Chanson de Berger, ou pieuse ou galante; amoureuse ou pastorale."[4] De la Croix ascribes no crudeness to the form, but implies by his wording that the form (as was indeed the case) had been cultivated. Certainly Passerat's villanelles, and those of the Pléiade poets, cannot be thought of as "popular" poetry or as, in any real sense, "les gestes des mutins." De la Croix's observations do not necessarily indicate, however, that he thought of "J'ai perdu" as a fixed-form paradigm. Subsequent prosodic texts do not recognize Passerat's villanelle as the formal model until fairly late in the nineteenth century.[5]

In some of the nineteenth-century texts on prosody there is another possible explanation for the relegation of the villanelle to temporary oblivion, and that is the reluctance to grant the tercet's status as a strophe. In his *Enseignement méthodique de la versification française* (4th ed., 1859), Auguste Carion writes: "On trouve encore des stances de trois vers qu'on appelle *tercets*; mais on ne peut les employer seules pour une piece: il faut les joindre à des stances d'un plus grand nombre de vers."[6]

Similarly, Gustave Weigand argues that "Les stances de trois vers (*tercet*), très fréquentes en italien, n'ont pas été adoptés par l'usage, comme trop courtes pour former un entrelacement de rimes."[7] As late as 1911, Philippe Martinon asks, "Mais le tercet fait-il une strophe?"[8] Although the Middle Ages recognized the tercet, notably in the *terza rima*, Martinon considers the tercet a dubious strophe at best, and agrees with the conventional view that "la strophe la plus courte est le quatrain" (p. 89).

A more important factor delaying the revival of the villanelle, however, is the several limitations of the form itself. By the end of the nineteenth century the villanelle was being mentioned in prosodic texts, but as Clair Tisseur observes, the "ron-ron revenant" which can delight the ear can also lead to abuses.[9] Of Maurice Rollinat's "L'Orniere," in 28 stanzas, Tisseur says: "Au dixième couplet l'envie vous prenait d'étrangler la poete" (p. 318). L. E. Kastner's comments as to the trifling nature of the form, preferring Passerat's to any of the nineteenth-century French efforts, including those more serious attempts of Leconte de Lisle, suggest that the villanelle lacks appeal, but he does not indicate the problems inherent in the form.[10] Warner F. Patterson, in his monumental study, *Three Centuries of French Poetic Theory* (1935), simply disregards the villanelle, with the virelay, as a poem of "lesser range and power" than the rondeau, the ballade, and the chant royal.[11]

To some extent the writers of villanelles are themselves responsible for the relegation of the form to triviality. Following Passerat, most of them have limited their subject matter to artificial moments in the pastoral drama. The relatively light seven- or eight-syllable line tends to predominate, the first and third lines of each stanza ending with a feminine rhyme and the second, masculine. Beyond that, however, among the French poets there is very little experimentation with the form, perhaps, in part, because the rhymes come easily enough in French. The need for slant or near rhyme and for eye rhyme has opened the form considerably for poets writing in English. The poet writing in English is severely challenged by the requisite seven "*a*" and six "*b*" rhyming words. Yet the limitations of the form are similar regardless of the language. Two lines, ultimately a couplet that must function as a unit, will be repeated four times each within a span (usually) of just nineteen lines. The revival of the villanelle would require that individual poets overcome the limitations of the form. The redundancy must either be concealed somehow, or it must be made to appear necessary.

Théodore de Banville's "Villanelle de Buloz," written in 1845, is indicative of the poet's tendency to reserve the form for playful subjects treated, in this case, with burlesque humor. Banville apparently deserves the credit (or the censure, depending upon one's perspective) for bringing Passerat's fixed-form villanelle back to life.[12] Théophile Gautier's irregular form "Villanelle rhythmique," written in 1837, attests to the renewal of interest in Renaissance forms prior to Banville's and Philoxène Boyer's return to Passerat. Gautier, Banville, and Boyer, along with another reviver of the villanelle, Leconte de Lisle, were all represented in the first *Parnasse contemporain* in 1866.

Before considering Banville's fixed-form villanelle, some attention should be given to Gautier's "Villanelle rhythmique" which, in subject matter and tone, resembles the work of the Pléiade poets. Among the revivers of the villanelle, as I will demonstrate, there is considerable variation as to application of the form when it comes to subject matter, tone, and context (i.e., "setting," but that term suggests a dramatic or narrative element which is sometimes inappropriate to the poem). A decision should eventually be reached as to the capability of the fixed-form villanelle to sustain the varied uses that are brought to it by the nineteenth-century practitioners. Gautier's poem is of some interest here, even though it is not written after Passerat's model, because it is similar in tenor to the villanelles of Passerat, and of Desportes, Du Bellay, and others.

Gautier's villanelle, in octosyllabic octets (*ababcdcd*) with a disyllabic concluding line, is a conventional idyll of a lover inviting his beloved at the coming of spring to gather flowers in the woods. The second of the three stanzas will serve to illustrate the almost précieux texture of the poem.

> Le printemps est venu, ma belle,
> C'est le mois des amants béni,
> Et l'oiseau, satinant son aile,
> Dit des vers au rebord du nid.
> Oh! viens donc sur le banc de mousse,
> Pour parler de nos beaux amours,
> Et dis-moi de ta voix si douce:
> Toujours![13]

Always the painter, Gautier writes an essentially visual poem. It was set to music by Xavier Boisselot. The poem is somewhat reminiscent of Du Bellay's "Villanelle" ("En ce moys délicieux"), but Gautier avoids the conventional ironic discrepancy between the season and the mistress, on the one hand, and himself, on the other, as voiced in Du Bellay's refrain: "Belle et franche Marguerite,/Pour vous j'ay ceste douleur."[14]

Banville's "Villanelle de Buloz" could hardly be more different from Gautier's and the villanelles of the Renaissance. At twenty-five lines, his fixed-form version is six lines longer than that of Passerat, but most prosodists agree that the number of stanzas in the fixed-form villanelle may very.[15] Banville's poem offers an interesting case of a satiric application of the form, proceeding, in fact, from a parody of Passerat:

> J'ai perdu mon Limayrac,
> Ce coup-là me bouleverse.
> Je veux me vêtir d'un sac.[16]

Buloz, the title character of the poem, was the publicist who built the *Revue des deux-mondes*, serving as editor in chief during the 1830's and 1840's. Poulin Limayrac, one of the outstanding literary journalists of the day, left the *Revue* in 1845, the year in which the poem was written. The topical nature of the poem and its playful colloquialism seem well suited to the light quality of the form:

> Sans son habile mic-mac,
> Sainte-Beuve tergiverse.
> Je veux me vêtir d'un sac.
>
> Il a pris son havresac,
> Et j'ai pris la fièvre tierce.
> J'ai perdu mon Limayrac.

Readers of the poem are probably not surprised to find that the resolution of Buloz' dilemma is in "cognac."

The villanelle seems also to be an appropriate form for Banville's "Villanelle des pauvres housseurs," a satiric attack on "Un tout petit pamphlétaire" whose piece published in *Figaro* (December 30, 1858) renders him open to attack as a lackey of Voltaire. The arrogant "university man" seems like "un marabout/Sur le fauteuil de Voltaire" (p. 149). None of what might be regarded as Banville's better poems, however, are villanelles. Charles Morice's *Choix de poésies* (Paris, 1923) of Banville's work includes none of his villanelles. Perhaps this is because Banville did not produce in his own villanelles a poem in keeping with his comment in his *Petit traité de poésie française* (1872), where he quotes Philoxène Boyer's "La Marquise Aurore," provides detailed rules of the form, and then remarks: "Et rien n'est plus chatoyant que ce petit poème.

On dirait une tresse formée de fils d'argent et d'or, que traverse un troisième fil, couleur de rose!"[17] Banville's villanelles may have offered some latitude to the subject matter and tone generally considered appropriate to the form; and while the villanelle in his hand remains something of a *joujou*, perhaps that is preferable to the *bijou d'étagère* that it becomes with Boyer and others.

Philoxène Boyer's villanelle, first published in *Les Deux saisons* in 1867, is almost insufferably laden with Pléiade-like artificiality, complete with shepherdess and mythological allusion. These are the first four stanzas of the 25-line poem:

> Près de Marie-Antoinette,
> Dans le petit Trianon,
> Fûtes-vous pas bergerettes?
>
> Vous a-t-on conté fleurette
> Aux bords du nouveau Lignon,
> Près de Marie-Antoinette?
>
> Des fleurs sur votre houlette,
> Un surnom sur votre nom,
> Fûtes-vous pas bergerettes?
>
> Etiez-vous noble soubrette,
> Comme Iris avec Junon,
> Près de Marie-Antoinette?[18]

In his *Camées parisiens* (1873), Banville refers to Boyer's high forehead as "lumineux plein de pensées, que semble éclairer la vision des choses éternelles."[19] Clearly the vision of Boyer in this poem, Juno and Iris to the contrary notwithstanding, is of the quotidian and the temporal. Lacking the humor of Banville and the easy simplicity of Passerat, Boyer nearly reduces the villanelle to saccharin. Passerat has no recourse to mythological deities or to historical names and places in "J'ai perdu ma tourterelle." His villanelle is a simple complaint of a lover, uncomplicated by the trappings of the shepherdess and emphasizing the direct emotions of the lover rather than the cleverness of the poet. Boyer's concluding hyperbole, to the effect that the Marquise Aurore's "simple cornette/Aurait converti Zénon," suggests a straining for wit (as also in lines 7–8 and 10–11 above) which conflicts with his attempt to associate the woman with flowers, simplicity, and generous behavior.

Perhaps inspired by the efforts of Banville and Boyer, or perhaps having read Banville's *Petit traité*, a very minor poet, Joseph Boulmier, produced in 1878 the first, and perhaps the only, collection of villanelles in French literature. But although Boulmier does mention the Parnassians in his 24-page introduction, he mentions none of them by name, and he devotes his comments almost entirely to Passerat. Very little of Boulmier's biography is available. Born at Tournus in 1821, a proofreader by profession, he identifies himself as a stereotypical Burgundian whose consolation is in wine, which leaves him never disconsolate but never rich. His first published work appears to have been a patriotic piece, *Jehan le Brave, ou la bataille de Poitiers* (Poitiers: F.-A. Saurin, 1845). He collaborated with Adolphe Royannez in writing a historical drama on Francis Villon in 1865 and with Eugene Vignon in a one-act verse drama, *L'Aveugle*, in 1879. Other work included a study of the seventeenth-century poet, Estienne Dolet, and three books of verse published between 1857 and 1868. His *Villanelles*, forty poems following the model of Passerat very closely (nineteen lines of seven syllables, feminine rhymes for the first and third lines of each tercet), were published in 1878, with a second printing in 1879. Thereafter, his name disappears from the literary record upon which, after all, he had not made a very large mark.

In his introduction to the *Villanelles* Boulmier surveys the etymology of the word and then offers as examples of the irregular form villanelle Philippe Desportes's "Rozette, pour une peu d'absence" and D'Urfé's "Villanelle d'Amidor reprochant une legereté" from the *Astrée*. He also quotes Passerat's irregular villanelle, "Qui en sa fantasie," which is a coarse jest of cuckoldry. Of the necessity for limiting the number of the stanzas to that preferred by Passerat, Boulmier writes: "Plus, ce serait trop: ou mettrait, du plomb aux ailes de ce léger poème."[20] It is especially important, he adds, that the refrain lines be recalled "d'une manière tellement exacte et naturelle que l'un quelconque des deux ne puisse pas, tout aussi bien, prendre la place de l'autre, et réciproquement" (p. 15). This, he confesses, he has sometimes been unable to avoid.

Unfortunately, one of the poems in which Boulmier took apparent special pride is his "Pour faire une villanelle," which he prints twice (pp. 16, 31–32). In this poem he offers rules of composition, insisting that "La méthode est simple et belle." In this way the writers of villanelles during the nineteenth century undercut their own work, and at the same time tend to restrict the potential of the villanelle as a form. Boulmier's influence on subsequent villanelles was probably not very great, but his work was known by one of the earliest popularizers of the villanelle in English, Andrew Lang.[21] To Lang and other early English writers of the villanelle, Boulmier passed along the view that the villanelle was easy to write, and therefore, implicitly, inconsequential.

One of Lang's contemporaries, W. E. Henley, provides an excellent example of the condescending attitude toward the form by the very poets who were attempting it.

> A dainty thing's the Villanelle
>   Sly, musical, a jewel in rhyme,
> It serves its purpose passing well.
>
> A double-clappered silver bell
>   That must be made to clink in chime,
> A dainty thing's the Villanelle;
>
> And if you wish to flute a spell,
>   Or ask a meeting 'neath the lime,
> It serves its purpose passing well.

At this point, approximately half-way through the poem, one can only wonder just what "purpose" Henley perceives for the villanelle. The phrase "to clink in chime" constitutes a rather desperate twist of idiom in order to produce rhyme and rhythm. Henley suggests that the villanelle is appealing musically, which may be reminiscent of the form's ultimate origin in sixteenth-century Italian music, but only in a rather frivolous fashion. Apparently it is also suited to dalliance.

> You must not ask of it the swell
>   Of organs grandiose and sublime —
> A dainty thing's the Villanelle;
>
> And, filled with sweetness, as a shell
>   Is filled with sound, and launched in time,
> It serves its purpose passing well.
>
> Still fair to see and good to smell
>   As in the quaintness of its prime,
> A dainty thing's the Villanelle,
> It serves its purpose passing well.[22]

In the latter portion of the poem, Henley's difficulty with the midline of the stanza continues. One must forgive an extra syllable in the eleventh line of the poem, or else quite consciously elide one (reading "grandiose" with a y-glide). Denying the villanelle any sublimity, Henley allows it merely "sweetness" and "quaintness." The reaching for the flower metaphor in the closing quatrain, which renders the villanelle "good to smell," is particularly disastrous. Ernest Dowson's "Villanelle of his Lady's

Treasures," which seems to borrow some of its language from Henley, is somewhat more successful because in using the villanelle as a metaphoric product of his mistress' beauty, Dowson creates a genuine vehicle for the poem.[23] Moreover, Dowson, unlike Henley and many other writers of villanelles, allows the use of slant or near rhymes (musical/well, virginal/well, possible/Villanelle). This practice gives him the flexibility that the form requires, especially in English, and it avoids the exact but forced rhyming that is observable in Henley's poem.

The apparent effortlessness with which a poet like Boulmier or his English followers, either direct or indirect, composes his villanelles might lead one to inquire whether the form is not deceptively simple. Once the poet commits himself to trivial subjects and light tones, the poems tend to flow all too easily. The form is undergoing no tension with the subject matter, and when that happens we have, not "sug'red sonnets," but "sacch'rined villanelles." The poet James Dickey tells a story of a little boy with a stammer who was trying to tell a policeman about a traffic accident. Two things are characteristic of what the boy was doing, Dickey concludes: first, he was trying to say something of utmost importance; and second, his speech was blocked. Dickey uses this incident to illustrate his split-line technique and also to demonstrate the proper relationship between form and substance in poetry.[24] When that which the poet is trying to say is not of "utmost importance," but is wilfully slight, virtually any form will serve. There will be nothing to impede the statement. While one might be tempted to conclude that in such cases there is ideal agreement between form and substance, the fact is that there is no issue; it is, strictly speaking, *nolo contendere*. An exactly opposite state of affairs obtains, however, in Dylan Thomas' renowned villanelle, "Do Not Go Gentle Into That Good Night," where the tremendous force of the statement strains against the narrow confines of the form.

As I've suggested, there is no strain in the villanelles of Boulmier. The titles alone tell a good part of the story: "Á mon chat Gaspard," "Primavera," "Pipe cassée," "Un Baiser," "Rossignol, Rossignolet," "Les Deux roses," et al. Perhaps one of Boulmier's most severe hindrances is his hyperconsciousness of the fact that he is not writing a poem, which he will attempt to shape as a villanelle, but that he is writing a villanelle. Thus, "Le Vieu ramier" begins by telling the reader that this poem, no matter what else it is or may be about, is a villanelle:

> Pour qui cette villanelle
> Sur un vieil air de hautbois?
> C'est pour vous, pour la plus belle. (p. 39)

Often, as in "Trahi," the difficulties of writing an effective villanelle become part of the poem, thus compromising any sense of dramatic presence for the reader:

> Trahi par une infidèle,
> Que faire? Que devenir?
> Tournons une villanelle. (p. 83)

Betrayed by the unfaithful mistress, the poet turns to the presumably more reliable (if only in its predictability) villanelle.

Writing of the villanelle, however, Jerome Beaty and William H. Matchett observe that "it is vital that the lines reappear as naturally as possible, and yet that the reappearance in differing contexts give new depth, range, or precision to the lines involved."[25] This requirement is virtually impossible to meet when the poet is so conscious of the form to which he has committed himself. This may be why some of the most effective fixed-form villanelles in English are those, like Thomas' or like Theodore Roethke's "The Waking," which are not labelled "villanelle" in their title. If the reader is given a signal to expect the repetition of the refrain lines, he may lose some of the delight of rediscovery which occurs upon the repetition of the familiar line in a different context. One should remember, of course, that the circumstances with the villanelle are not the same as those with a sonnet or with most other fixed forms of poetry. The element of surprise remains in a sonnet because the rhyming words will vary throughout the poem. Of course in a collection of villanelles, especially in a collection like Boulmier's, in which no divergence from the paradigm is permitted, the delight of rediscovery is ipso facto compromised.

Boulmier's villanelles generally revolve around his own existence, which one might describe as lonely and tedious. There are his cats, Coquette and Gaspard, and there is his pipe, his wine, and his poetry, but mostly there is himself, as in "En hiver," feeling sorry for himself: "Chaque jour, a mon visage/Le miroir dit: 'Pauvre vieux!' " (p. 88). When Gaspard dies there is the predictable poem, "Il n'est plus," followed by a gently comic "Oraison funèbre." One of Boulmier's more appealing efforts is "Un Banquet a Chloris," which has an attractive humor.

Vous êtes belle et bien faite,
J'en conviens sincerement;
Mais, vrai, l'on n'est pas plus bête!

Avec cela, fort coquette,
Oh! tout naturellement;
Vous êtes belle et bien faite!

Votre mine est grassouillette
Votre sourire est charmant;
Mais, vrai, l'on n'est pas plus bête!

Vous n'avez rien dans la tête,
Rien dans le coeur; seulement
Vous êtes belle et bien faite!

Qu'on vous aimerait, muette!
Las! vous parlez constamment;
Mais, vrai, l'on n'est pas plus bête!

Pour le jour de votre fête
Agréez ce compliment:
Vous êtes belle et bien faite;
Mais, vrai, l'on n'est pas plus bête. (pp. 75–76)

Judged by the standards suggested above for the repetition of the refrain lines, this poem fails. The decisive end-stopping that occurs in the second line of all but one stanza breaks the body of the stanza apart from the refrain, thus assuring that no new "depth, range, or precision" will come to the refrain as a result of the varied context. A similar condition, but with even more pronounced end-stoppage, occurs in Banville's "Villanelle de Buloz." There is also no evidence in Boulmier's volume of that subtle beauty recommended by Banville in his *Petit traité*.

Boulmier's concluding villanelle, "Soyons franc," is a defensive manifesto to the effect that his book is not intended for the reader, but for himself. He lashes out against "l'Institut cacochyme," which is also the object of his wrath in "Profession de foi." In the latter, Boulmier declares himself opposed to grandiloquent expression, and, "Pareil à l'enfant qui jase,/Je rimaille en liberté" (p. 99). In this, he succeeded all too well.

Of considerably greater interest are the two villanelles, each taking slight liberties with Passerat's model, by Leconte de Lisle. "Le Temps, l'Étendue et le Nombre," which appeared in his *Poèmes tragiques* (1884), is two tercets shorter than the Passerat form and is octosyllabic. The extra syllable may add somewhat to the seriousness of the poem, and the reduction in the number of refrain lines definitely does. The repeated nasals [ã] and [c̃] create a hollowness which contributes greatly to the mood evoked. The epigraph is: "Une nuit noire, par un calme, sous l'Équateur."

Le Temps, l'Étendue et le Nombre
Sont tombés du noir firmament
Dans la mer immobile et sombre.

Suaire de silence et d'ombre,
La nuit efface absolument
Le Temps, l'Étendue et le Nombre.

Tel qu'un lourd et muet décombre,
L'Esprit plonge au vide dormant,
Dans la mer immobile et sombre.

En lui-même, avec lui, tout sombre,
Souvenir, rêve, sentiment,
Le Temps, l'Étendue et le Nombre,
Dans la mer immobile et sombre.[26]

This is apparently the first French villanelle to adopt a tone and to proceed from an atmosphere that is neither frivolous, burlesque, nor pastoral. It might be called a mood piece. It is charged with an ominous presentiment of utter annihilation; but an eerie silence prevails, as if the end of time, space, and being were like a becalmed ship on a dark tropical night, and not a fiery holocaust. The consonance of the [m] and [n] sounds deadens the entire poem and adds to its heaviness.

Leconte de Lisle's second villanelle, "Dans l'air léger," published first in the *Derniers poèmes* (1895), follows the Passerat model closely, though it is octosyllabic, until the last stanza. There, Leconte de Lisle concludes with a tercet rather than a quatrain, changes the rhyme pattern, and then concludes by repeating the first line of the poem. It is reminiscent in several ways of Banville's advice in the *Petit traité* concerning threads of gold and silver, and a third the color of rose. It seems almost a companion piece, for contrast, to "Le Temps."

Dans l'air léger, dans l'azur rose,
Un grêle fil d'or rampe et luit
Sur les mornes que l'aube arrose.

Much of the body of the poem seems in keeping with the almost précieux inclinations of so many writers of the villanelle, though the sharpness of image and range of diction is far superior to that of such a poet as Boulmier:

L'abeille boit ton âme, ô rose!
L'épasi tamarinier bruit
Sur les mornes que l'aube arrose.

It is the concluding tercet, however, that is the most engaging moment
in the poem:

Mais les yeux divins que j'aimais
Se sont fermés, et pour jamais,
Dans l'air léger, dans l'azur rose! (p. 288)

It is only in this stanza that the speaker introduces what has been on his
mind, apparently, from the first. Everything in the poem is opening,
shining, rising, flying. The poem is filled with active, present tense
verbs (rampe, luit, arrose, éclose, s'eveille, vole, fuit, boit, bruit, palpite,
ose, s'épanouit, repose, fait monter) until the last stanza, where the
imperfect and the *passé composé* suddenly appear to announce that his
beloved is dead. The effect, heightened by the wordplay *j'aimais/jamais*
and the disruption of the expected rhyme scheme, is striking. Leconte
de Lisle plays on the reader's expectations of the conventional villanelle,
seeming to satisfy those expectations, but only up to a point. The first
five tercets might be seen as an elaborate ruse to set up the reader for
the painful and, in several ways, disharmonious conclusion. The fact
that the eyes, again drawing from the conventional language of hyperbolic flattery, are "yeux *divins*," heightens still more the sense of incon-
gruity. The naturalistic, animal and physical world thrives, but the
divine mistress is dead, "et pour jamais." The last refrain line, which is
the first line of the poem, now rings painfully and bitterly ironic.

In part because he is willing to manipulate the form to some degree,
while not altering it radically, Leconte de Lisle produces what are probably the best villanelles written in French during the century. In bringing alternative subjects, contexts, and tones to the form, he is able to
broaden its potential. No one would deny, of course, that his villanelles
are superior to those of a Boulmier simply because Leconte de Lisle is a
vastly more talented poet. It is perhaps axiomatic that the true poet will
dare what the slavish imitator, hoping for security in conformity, will
not. At any rate, with Leconte de Lisle the villanelle achieves a range of
expression that frees it from the shackles of daintiness, frivolity, and
triviality. Moreover, his handling of the refrain lines is in keeping with
the advice of prosodists that fresh energy or varied perspective should
be supplied as they are repeated.

With Maurice Rollinat (1846–1903) the potential of the villanelle was to be further expanded. Like Leconte de Lisle an admirer of George Sand, Rollinat was the son of the deputy from Indre to the Constituent assembly. His first volume of poems, *Dans les brandes* (1877), was ignored. The single villanelle in that book, "Mon épinette," is similar to the conventional type as written by Boulmier, though already showing the characteristic Rollinat modification of the form— considerable expansion beyond the 19-line model of Passerat. It was Rollinat's next volume, *Les Névroses* (1883), influenced by his absorption in the works of Poe and Baudelaire, that established for him the small reputation that he still possesses. The subdivisions of that volume indicate a good deal about the contents: Ames, Luxures, Refuges, Spectres, Ténèbres. Rollinat wrote seventeen villanelles, which are scattered throughout his works, varying in length from 31 to 62 lines. No other poet has so cultivated the form, and no other poet has so openly defied the generally recognized limitations of the form. Readers of Rollinat's villanelles must finally decide whether the redundancy of the refrain lines is tedious or, as the poet apparently hoped, somehow incantatory.

The only way to gauge such a response is, of course, to read one of Rollinat's villanelles in its entirety. "La Buveuse d'absinthe," which I am reproducing below, is of moderate length for Rollinat, 49 lines, and is one of his most powerful efforts.

Elle était toujours enceinte,
Et puis elle avait un air . . .
Pauvre buveuse d'absinthe!

Elle vivait dans la crainte
De son ignoble partner:
Elle était toujours enceinte!

Par les nuits où le ciel suinte,
Elle couchait en plein air.
Pauvre buveuse d'absinthe!

Ceux que la débauche éreinte
La lorgnaient d'un oeil amer:
Elle était toujours enceinte!

Dans Paris, ce labyrinthe
Immense comme la mer,
Pauvre buveuse d'absinthe,

Elle allait, prunelle éteinte,

Rampant aux murs comme un ver . . .
Elle était toujours enceinte!

Oh! cette jupe déteinte
Qui se bombait chaque hiver!
Pauvre buveuse d'absinthe!

Sa voix n'etait qu'une plainte,
Son estomac qu'un cancer:
Elle était toujours enceinte!

Quelle farouche complainte
Dira son hideux spencer!
Pauvre buveuse d'absinthe!

Je la revois, pauvre Aminte,
Comme se c'était hier:
Elle était toujours enceinte!

Elle effrayait maint et mainte
Rien qu'en tournait sa cuiller;
Pauvre buveuse d'absinthe!

Quand elle avait une quinte
De toux, — Oh! qu'elle a souffert,
Elle était toujours enceinte! —

Elle ralait: Ça m'esquinte!
Je suis déjà dans l'enfer.
Pauvre buveuse d'absinthe.

Or elle but une pinte
De l'affreux liquide vert:
Elle était toujours enceinte!

Et l'agonie était peinte
Sur son oeil a peine ouvert;
Pauvre buveuse d'absinthe!

Quand son amant dit sans feinte:
D'ébarras, c'en est un fier!
Elle était toujours enceinte.
Pauvre buveuse d'absinthe![27]

In depicting the ugliness of the woman's existence, Rollinat suc-
ceeds in creating a sense of prevailing disease and inescapability. The
word "enceinte" perhaps retains both of its meanings in this poem, both
"pregnant" and "encircled" or "enclosed." Paris is a labyrinth from which
there is no escape short of death. Above her, the sky oozes, drips like

blood from an open wound. She is reduced not simply to something less than human, but to a worm, and the life within her is seen not as a fetus but as a cancer. The repeated comment, "Elle était toujours enceinte," is uttered not only by the poet outside the poem (as a commentator on her fate), but also by the poet as he inserts himself into the poem (11.28–30), and by others (11.10– 12) who leer unsympathetically at her condition, and finally by her smirking "lover" (11.46–49). It is this line of the refrain which comes closest to meeting the demand most modern prosodists make of the villanelle: "la maniere de dire le refrain devra varier: le changement d'intonation, le déplacement de l'accent d'intensité, l'introduction ou la suppression de pauses a l'intérieur du vers suffiront à modifier l'ambiance et donneront du charme à la villanelle."[28]

If Rollinat was not much concerned with the "charme" of his villanelles, he was certainly concerned with their musical qualities. He composed music which he sang with some of his poems, often performing at the Chat-Noir, the favorite cabaret of the *Hydropathes*, of which he may be considered a charter member. One of his most ambitious compositions, and probably the best known of his villanelles, "La Villanelle du Diable," was set as a "fantasie symphonique pour grand orchestre et orgue" by Charles M. T. Loeffler (Opus 9, 1905). And so the villanelle, despite Henley's warning against its use for "organs grandiose and sublime," gained a measure of respectability in the midst of its revival.

The "Villanelle du Diable," which has been translated into German by Stefan Zweig as "Die Teufelsritornell," is dedicated to Theodore de Banville. Like Boulmier and other strict adherents to Passerat's model, Rollinat generally writes a seven-syllable line:

> L'Enfer brûle, brûle, brûle,
> Ricaneur au timbre clair,
> Le Diable rôde et circule.
>
> Il guette, avance ou recule
> En zigzags, comme l'éclair;
> L'Enfer brûle, brûle, brûle.
>
> Dans le bouge et la cellule,
> Dans les caves et dans l'air
> Le Diable rôde et circule.
>
> Il se fait fleur, libellule,

> Femme, chat noir, serpent vert;
> L'Enfer brûle, brûle, brûle. (p. 323)

Throughout the poem Rollinat sustains the Baudelairean imagery in stressing the universality of the Devil's malignity:

> Lá, flottant comme une bulle,
> Ici, rampant comme un ver,
> Le Diable rôde et circule. (p. 324)

The connection between Rollinat's spirit of evil and the traditional Christian or Faustian lore is fairly vague and general. The Devil pierces each soul with his bitter insinuations; he mocks without scruple; he makes the good seem ridiculous, the old appear foolish:

> Chez le prêtre et l'incrédule
> Dont il veut l'âme et la chair,
> Le Diable rôde et circule. (p. 325)

In the concluding quatrain, the speaker envisions himself in a potentially Faustian predicament as midnight sounds: "Si j'allais voir Lucifer?" But he does not imply any sort of resolution. The answer to his question is merely the repetition of the haunting refrain, now appearing as a couplet: "L'Enfer brûle, brûle, brûle;/Le Diable rôde et circule."

In fact, most of Rollinat's villanelles might be said to be haunted, at least by the spirit of Baudelaire, as the titles suggest: "L'Orniere," "Pluie dans un ravin," "Mademoiselle Squelette," "Villanelle du ver de terre," "Les Poisons," "Les Deux revenants," "L'Étang du mauvais pas," et al. The Gothic sort of narrative line in "Les Deux revenants" is very close to Poe, or perhaps to Bürger's "Lenore." Those titles that are not foreboding in some way are generally misleading. "Le Baby," for example, gives a painful account of an infant's death:

> Un jour on me dit: Il tousse.
> Pourtant, chétif et perclus,
> Le baby suçait son pouce. (p. 225)

"Le Bonne rivière" turns out to be "la rivière des crapauds."[29] At the same time, the villanelle, although remaining somewhat restricted in range among English poets (Henley, Dowson, Dobson, Wilde, et al.), was finding a darker and more serious side in the poems of the young American poet, Edwin Arlington Robinson.[30]

Since the end of the nineteenth century, the villanelle has had a fairly strong and steady growth among poets writing in English. Versifiers and poetasters continue to pursue the pastoral, trivial, or frivolous modes. But if the form has had its Clinton Scollards, its "Poetry is Fun" adherents, its news columnists (Delos Avery, Bert Taylor), and its whimsy anthologizers in England and the United States, it has also remained attractive to serious and able poets, both known and unknown. Aside from Ezra Pound's irregular form "Villanelle: The Psychological Hour" (1915) and the fixed-form villanelle by Joyce in *A Portrait of the Artist as a Young Man* (1916), there are examples by Robinson, Thomas, and Roethke, already cited, and by Elizabeth Bishop, W. H. Auden, William Empson, Gilbert Sorrentino, John Wain, Richard Eberhart, Sylvia Plath, Richard Hugo, James Merrill, Carolyn Kizer, Marilyn Hacker, and many other well-known poets. Certainly among English and American poets the revival of the villanelle in the mid-nineteenth century in France has been important. Among contemporary French poets, the present status of the form is more difficult to ascertain. It seems to be less attractive, perhaps because the form is more familiar and more accessible than it is to poets writing in English. Certainly the villanelle survives in twentieth-century French poetry. There is, for example, Max Jacob's irregular form "Villonelle" (1921) and Louis Aragon's "Villanelle: Au bord des fontaines" (1926), also irregular and perhaps a parody of the fixed-form type. Marc Du Bressis includes three fixed-form villanelles after Leconte de Lisle's truncated 13-line model in his *Amour et poésie* (1969). The future of the villanelle, however, appears to belong to poets who are facing the challenges which the form offers to the English language.

♦

4.
The Villanelle in English:
1874–1922

The Victorian Villanelle

The Aesthetic movement of the latter third of the nineteenth century in England brought to late Victorian poetry a much needed "literary cosmopolitanism."[1] The English Parnassians, following such French progenitors as Leconte de Lisle and Théodore de Banville, offered an alternative to the generally utilitarian Philistinism which dominated the literary scene, and they reestablished literary relations with France. Of the opposition to the Aesthetic movement, James K. Robinson writes: "Most poets shared the general English dislike of French political institutions and found the dogma of art for art's sake incompatible with one of art for morality's sake."[2] While the Parnassian and Symbolist commitment to *art pour l'art* was not to be shared altogether by subsequent poets in England and the United States, the sensibility was significantly influenced; to such a degree, one might say, that the exact influence is impossible to determine.

The problem of influence is complicated by the fact that few English poets who were prominent between 1870 and 1900 are read today. Edmund Gosse, Andrew Lang, William Henley, John Payne — these names are nearly absent from anthologies now, and not altogether unjustifiably. Robinson notes the understandable confusion of Austin Dobson with Alfred Austin and Ernest Dowson.[3] From the shower of French fixed forms which rained down, only the villanelle (and to a lesser extent, the sestina) retains significant popularity.[4] Some reconsideration of the late Victorian villanelle, therefore, may reveal those qualities which have led to its adoption as perhaps the favorite fixed form, except for the sonnet, in English and American poetry.

With the publication of two villanelles by Théodore de Banville in his *Odes funambulesques* (1857), Jean Passerat's form, exemplified in "J'ai perdu ma tourterelle" (ca. 1590), was readmitted to French poetry. In his *Petit traité de poésie francais* (1872), as indicated in the previous chapter, Banville ushered in the form by quoting an example by Philoxene Boyer and providing the "rules": division into tercets, the first and third lines using feminine rhyme, the second masculine; no fixed number of tercets; the first and third lines of the first tercet to alternate as refrain lines in succeeding tercets until coming together at the end of the poem in a quatrain.[5] Later practitioners were to return to the rigid 19-line form of Passerat, and especially in rhyme-poor English, the feminine rhymes have generally been disregarded.

When Edmund Gosse's "A Plea for Certain Exotic Forms of Verse" was published in the *Cornhill Magazine* in 1877, he could cite only his own poem, which appeared three years earlier in the *Athenaeum*, as an example of the villanelle in English.[6] Within ten years, however, his lone villanelle had considerable company. Warning against the excesses of the "Spasmodic School" which followed Keats, Gosse compares current poetic license to a sculptor affixing a plaster nose to a marble statue. He cautions against form filled with inadequate matter; but better that, Gosse complains, than "to desert rhythm and metre altogether, and adopt the uncouth prose in which a certain American rhapsodist clothes his prophetic utterances." He concludes: "I hope I may be dead before the English poets take Walt Whitman for their model in style" (p. 71).

The villanelle Gosse considers to be among the "more elaborate and serious" of the new forms, and one "for which a pathetic or passionate rendering seems almost imperative" (p. 64). This view is directly opposed to that of such prosodists as Calvin S. Brown who, in noting the artificiality of the form, writes: "A passionate or vehement villanelle would be an impossibility."[7] Within three years of Brown's statement, Dylan Thomas' renowned "Do Not Go Gentle into That Good Night" had been published, but Brown's reservations, founded upon his knowledge of such early efforts as Oscar Wilde's "Theocritus," deserve some inquiry. Gosse advises that the newly introduced fixed forms "should be attractive in spite of, and not because of, their difficulty," and he adds that the true test of the poem's success is that the reader is given "an impression of spontaneity and ease" (p. 71). Such demands are perhaps more difficult to satisfy with the villanelle than with any other fixed form of poetry, primarily because, as Brown observes, the villanelle is more "conspicuous."

Gosse's pioneer villanelle, "Wouldst Thou Not Be Content to Die," offers a good example of the problems faced by the poet using the relatively limited array of English rhymes. He complicates his task when he surpasses Passerat's 19-line length, thus running the risk of boring or anesthetizing his reader with the redundant refrain lines. Few poets writing in English have followed Gosse's decision to extend the length of the villanelle, and Gosse himself cut the poem by two tercets in later printings of his work. The length is relatively slight, however, beside the 62-line efforts of the French poet, Maurice Rollinat. Surprisingly, no early writers of the villanelle in English, so far as I can tell, relaxed the standards of Passerat and followed the lead of Leconte de Lisle in his 13-line villanelle, "Le Temps, l'Étendue et le Nombre."

Although a strict adherence to the practices of the French villanelle would require feminine rhymes for the first and third lines of each tercet, Gosse goes further than most poets writing in English when he uses feminine rhyme for the middle lines. Unfortunately, this decision limits severely his range of rhymes and leaves the poem "-inging." Such a lively element of sound in a poem devoted to the sober thoughts of passing autumn and approaching death seems inconsistent with the intended tone:

Wouldst thou not be content to die
  When low-hung fruit is hardly clinging,
And golden Autumn passes by?

If we could vanish, thou and I,
  While the last woodland bird is singing,
Wouldst thou not be content to die?

Deep drifts of leaves in the forest lie,
  Red vintage that the frost is flinging,
And golden Autumn passes by.

Beneath this delicate rose-gray sky,
  Whilst sunset bells are faintly ringing,
Wouldst thou not be content to die?

For wintry webs of mist on high
  Out of the muffled earth are springing,
And golden Autumn passes by.

For the "*a*" rhyme, which must be repeated seven times in Passerat's model and nine times in this poem, Gosse chooses one of the most abundantly occurring syllables in English. Only five or six other combinations, as a rhyming dictionary will demonstrate, would provide a greater number of rhyming words. Staying as he does with pure rhyme, Gosse is limited in his range, but he does not resort to such inversions as that in line 7 (above) very often. When he is able to produce some music, as in line 11, "For wintry webs of mist on high," the effect is compromised by the insistent end-rhymes which, as in this case, sometimes clash with the soft vowel sounds within the lines.

At line 16 Gosse heightens the urgency of the questioning process by use of an apostrophe, and the poem concludes with a more forceful declarative statement. Previous responses to the questions, in the third and fifth tercets, have simply elaborated the visual imagery of approaching winter. The concluding declaration, extending over two stanzas, personifies winter as a man, aiming the statement not toward the fading autumn, but toward the supposed listener whose identity is connected with the female "life" (1 23):

> O now when pleasures fade and fly,
> And Hope her southward flight is winging,
> Wouldst thou not be content to die?
>
> Lest Winter come, with wailing cry,
> His cruel icy bondage bringing,
> When golden Autumn hath passed by,
>
> And thou, with many a tear and sigh,
> While life her wasted hands is wringing,
> Shalt pray in vain for leave to die
> When golden Autumn hath passed by. (p. 65)

The change in the second refrain line to the past tense stresses the urgency of the situation, as does the considerably altered first refrain line.

The pathos of this villanelle is similar to that of James Joyce's "Are You Not Weary of Ardent Ways?" in *A Portrait of the Artist as a Young Man* (1916), but one scarcely misses the second and third stanzas when they are deleted from later printings of the poem. It might be argued that the "woodland bird" of line 5 sets up the metaphor of Hope "winging" south in line 17, but for the most part the poem is conventional in sentiment and essentially descriptive or pictorial in mode. Despite the implied presence of another person, no genuine dramatic moment occurs in the poem, nor is there any inner tension on the part of the speaker. Certain elements of Gosse's art, however, should be credited. Unlike some of his followers, he does allow some variation in the refrain lines, and he moves fairly naturally from the second line of each stanza (without excessively pronounced end punctuation) to the refrain line; the penultimate tercet moves easily into the concluding stanza. Moreover, the concluding couplet stands up as a unit, not as a pair of isolated lines compelled to be together.

The English poets whose villanelles soon followed Gosse's effort brought various metrical maneuverings, but for the most part their poems followed the point of view and tone implied by the adjectives which are prominent in his comments on the villanelle: precious, delicate, dainty. "It requires a peculiar mood and moment" to compose a villanelle, Gosse writes (p. 64), and for many writers that mood and moment involved some form of nostalgia for the Golden Age (often pastoral), for past love, or for passing time (*fin de siècle*, as often as not). Too often, as subsequent examples will demonstrate, the result is a sort of insipid pathos, a sentimentality which is not capable of being poignant, however it may try.

Austin Dobson's "When I Saw You Last, Rose," for example, which Brander Matthews describes as "an alluring portrayal of fascinating maidenhood limned with the assured swiftness of an etching,"[8] could hardly be more banal. The concluding stanzas give some indication of the poem's superficiality:

> In your bosom it shows
> There's a guest on the sly;
> (How fast the time goes!)
>
> Is it Cupid? Who knows?
> Yet you used not to sigh,
> When I saw you last, Rose; —
> How fast the time goes![9]

While it would be unfair to judge any villanelle solely by its concluding lines, Mary J. J. Wrinn is probably correct in advising that the poet must first plan the couplet which will end the poem and will provide the refrain lines. One line, as she notes, "should grow out of the other."[10] If the couplet does not have some peculiar force or appeal, the poem will likely fail. In this villanelle, Dobson works the obvious metaphor from the title character's name, in which the woman, once but a bud, is now in bloom. Throughout the poem the last line ("How fast. . .") is set aside each time it acts as a refrain, whereas the other refrain line ("When I saw . . . ") is worked naturally into each tercet. In effect, then, only the last line of the concluding couplet has developed independent status, and in this case, that line is not especially impressive. One attractive feature of this villanelle is Dobson's metrical play. Gosse uses a fairly conventional iambic tetrameter which is roughly comparable to the seven- or eight-syllable lines that predominate in the French villanelle (hendecasyllables and hexameters are the most common line length in the Renaissance Italian villanelle). As Matthews states, "the felicity of the meter, anapestic dimeter," contributes to the simplicity and delicacy of Dobson's poem. The virtues of simplicity and delicacy, however, soon wear thin.

In his other villanelles, Dobson tries various measures (anapestic trimeter, iambic tetrameter and trimeter, mixtures of iambs and anapests), but the range of tone stays between that of "When I Saw You Last, Rose" and Gosse's "Wouldst Thou Not." "On a Nankin Plate," for example, is a little *jeu d'esprit* on a man who loved too late: "Ah me, but it might have been!" (p. 483). "Tu Ne Quaesieris" is a somewhat similar poem, at least in tone, to "Wouldst Thou Not." The concluding couplet, following the lament that "churl Time is flying," pretty well tells the story: "Seek not, O Maid, to know/When thou and I must go" (p. 485). The poem seems in some ways to be a projection of Gosse's, seizing upon a mild *carpe diem* approach to the passage of time rather than a more quietly stoic sort of acceptance. Just as "When I Saw You" and "On a Nankin Plate" are nostalgic poems on passing time and lost love, "When This Old World Was New" is a nostalgic paeon to the Golden Age, when "Love was a shepherd too."[11]

One of Dobson's most interesting efforts may have initiated a small round of villanelles concerning Theocritus by Oscar Wilde and Andrew Lang. Dobson's "For a Copy of Theocritus," perhaps of Herbert Snow's (later Kynaston) *Theocritus*, which went through its third edition at the Clarendon Press in 1877, sets the tone:

> O Singer of the field and fold,
> Theocritus! Pan's pipe was thine, —
> Thine was the happier Age of Gold.
>
> For thee the scent of new-turned mould,
> The bee-hives, and the murmuring pine,

O Singer of the field and fold!

Thou sang'st the simple feasts of old, —
The beechen bowl made glad with wine . . .
Thine was the happier Age of Gold.

Thou bad'st the rustic loves be told, —
Thou bad'st the tuneful reeds combine,
O Singer of the field and fold!

And round thee, ever-laughing, rolled
The blithe and blue Sicilian brine . . .
Thine was the happier Age of Gold.

Alas for us! Our songs are cold;
Our Northern suns too sadly shine: —
O Singer of the field and fold,
Thine was the happier Age of Gold![12]

From the first tercet (line 3) the implied comparison that is made explicit in the concluding stanza is urged. This sentiment — that late nineteenth-century England has need of a certain pagan vigor and Mediterranean passion — is echoed in Oscar Wilde's "Pan — A Villanelle":

O Goat-foot God of Arcady!
   Cyllene's shrine is grey and old;
This northern isle hath need of thee![13]

Dobson emphasizes the simple, natural life of the Theocritan pastoral — farmland, beehives, forests, beechwood bowls of wine for the plain feasts, reeds for music, all encompassed by the sea.

Oscar Wilde's "Theocritus," published in 1881, appears to owe something to Dobson's poem from the first line, but if his beginning, "O Singer . . . ," is imitative of Dobson, the remainder of the line, "of Persephone," identifies his departure. Wilde focuses on the evocative power of names encountered in the poems of Theocritus: Amaryllis, Simaetha, Hecate, Polyphemus, Daphnis, Lacon. He retains Dobson's bee and the sea, which becomes "light and laughing" rather than "ever-laughing" and "blithe."

O Singer of Persephone!
   In the dim meadows desolate
Dost thou remember Sicily?

Still through the ivy flits the bee
   Where Amaryllis lies in state;
O Singer of Persephone!

Simaetha calls on Hecate
   And hears the wild dogs at the gate;
Dost thou remember Sicily?

Still by the light and laughing sea
   Poor Polypheme bemoans his fate;
O Singer of Persephone!

And still in boyish rivalry
   Young Daphnis challenges his mate;
Dost thou remember Sicily?

Slim Lacon keeps a goat for thee,
   For thee the jocund shepherds wait;
O Singer of Persephone!
Dost thou remember Sicily?[14]

The most important difference between the two poems is in the matter of thematic statement and tone. The "field and fold" of Dobson's poem is associated with an age of innocence. The very fact that Wilde's Theocritus is addressed as "Singer of Persephone" indicates a dark under-current, and the fields from which Persephone was abducted by Hades are described as "dim" and "desolate." Amaryllis is dead. The sensual, jilted Simaetha (Idyll II) visits the goddess of sorcery and the underworld in order to regain her departed lover. Polyphemus (Idyll XI) bewails his inability to win the affections of Galatea. Wilde's allusion to Daphnis, however, is apparently to the eighth idyll, in which he bests his companion, Menalcas, in a singing match, and not to the first idyll, which recounts his wasting away because of an unsuccessful amour. The contentious Lacon (Idyll V), the shepherd, loses his contest with the goatherd Comatas, so why Wilde suggests Lacon awaiting Theocritus with a goat, unless he has misread the poem, is unclear.[15] Whatever the cause, Wilde's intention appears to be to end the poem on a positive note.

    Andrew Lang's "Villanelle: To Lucia," first published in 1881 and, like those of Dobson and Wilde, written in iambic tetrameter, remains a tribute to the pastoral age of Theocritus rather than a lament (as with Dobson) of the present. Like Dobson's, however, Lang's vision of the pastoral age detects no death or misery; although unlike Dobson, Lang relates the craft of Theocritus to Apollo rather than Pan. The choice of Apollo over Pan, whose temperament is less stable and whose connections with fertility are more marked, perhaps contributes to the lighter quality of Lang's rendition.

> Apollo left the golden Muse
>   And shepherded a mortal's sheep,
> Theocritus of Syracuse!
>
> To mock the giant swain that woos
>   The sea-nymph in the sunny deep,
> Apollo left the golden Muse.
>
> Afield he drove his lambs and ewes,
>   Where Milon and where Battus reap,
> Theocritus of Syracuse!
>
> To watch thy tunny-fishers cruise
>   Below the dim Sicilian steep
> Apollo left his golden Muse.
>
> Ye twain did loiter in the dews,
>   Ye slept the swain's unfever'd sleep,
> Theocritus of Syracuse!
>
> That Time might half with *his*confuse
>   Thy songs, — like his, that laugh and leap, —
> Theocritus of Syracuse,
>   Apollo left the golden Muse![16]

Lang's poem is, of the three, the most devoted to commemorating Theocritus himself. In tone it seems to fall somewhere between the two. His allusions in lines 4 and 8 to the "giant swain" (Polyphemus) and to Milon and Battus (Idylls X and IV) are essentially window dressing. Dobson uses no such references to personages in the idylls, while they are quite important to Wilde's poem. Dobson's "blithe and blue Sicilian brine" and Wilde's "light and laughing sea" becomes first "the sunny deep" and then "the dim Sicilian steep" in Lang's villanelle, suggesting a greater inclination toward the epithet here. Lang is most successful at reintroducing the refrain "with slightly different significations" while leaving the words unchanged, a requirement of the well-turned villanelle in both French and English.[17] It is this criterion that has been most often and most successfully challenged by later writers of the villanelle, and those writers who have followed Gosse's lead have generally produced more effective poems as a result of the added flexibility. The only significant variation on the form here is in Lang's arrangement to the quatrain, in which the usual refrain order (line 1, line 3) is reversed, as if the confusion of Apollo's with Theocritus's poetry were reflected in Lang's concluding couplet. The relatively light punctuation of the second lines in each tercet (usually commas are sufficient) indicates a fairly easy movement into the refrain lines throughout the poem.

Lang's villanelle addressed to Joseph Boulmier, the minor French poet whose *Villanelles* (1878) is the first collection in French or English, compares the present state of the form to the autumn of "Fading leaf and falling fruit" (p. 172), and so joins those poems by Gosse and by Dobson lamenting the passing of time and the approach of death-dealing winter. While the melancholy of these poems is not to be compared with the Cavalier dejection of such poems as Lovelace's "The Grasshopper" or Herrick's "To Blossoms," the *fin de siècle* atmosphere is pervasive.

The same may be said for W. E. Henley's villanelle, "Where's the Use of Sighing" (1888). Written in trochaic trimeter, this poem is of interest only as a metrical toy. The first two stanzas exemplify not only the cliched language that prevails throughout the poem, but also Henley's use of anadiplosis as an added repetitive device (used three times in the poem, where the third refrain line appears). This device might have admitted of some appeal in a poem of greater attractions in other respects.

> Where's the use of sighing?
>   Sorrow as you may,
> Time is always flying—
>
> Flying!—and defying
>   Men to say him nay . . .
> Where's the use of sighing?[18]

Throughout the poem, Henley is unable to perform variations in nuance of meaning in the refrain lines, and his feminine rhymes (as in Dobson's "Tu Ne Quaesieris"), along with the short line length, make subtlety or apparent spontaneity of the refrain impossible. When he must resort to "Men with by-and-bying" in order to get his rhyme, Henley loses any opportunity to sustain a tone of serious melancholy.

Of all the early writers of the villanelle in English, Henley, in fact, seems most willing, if not determined, to limit the form to triviality. He says as much in "A Dainty Thing's the Villanelle" (p. 228; see Chapter 3, pp. 67–68), a poem which Brander Matthews describes as a "labored effort" to be "airy."[19] Henley is better when he attempts a comic application of the form:

Now ain't they utterly too-too
 (She ses, my Missus mine, ses she)
Them flymy little bits of Blue.

Joe, just you kool 'em — nice and skew
 Upon our old meogginee,
Now ain't they utterly too-too?

They're better than a pot'n' a screw,
 They're equal to a Sunday spree,
Them flymy little bits of Blue!

Suppose I put 'em up the flue,
 And booze the profits, Joe? Not me.
Now ain't they utterly too-too?

I do the 'Igh Art fake, I do.
 Joe, I'm consummate, and I *see*
Them flymy little bits of Blue.

Which, Joe, is why I ses to you —
 Aesthetic-like, and limp, and free —
Now *ain't* they utterly too-too,
Them flymy little bits of Blue?[20]

In this satire on the Aesthetic movement, Henley's cockney couple wage an indirect debate (we hear the wife's voice as reported by her husband) over the "flymy" (artful) "bits of Blue" (the blue china which was much prized at the time[21]). It is quite possible, in fact, that the poem is an indirect attack on Oscar Wilde, whom Henley supported for membership in the Savile Club in 1888, but toward whom he was unable to remain amicable.[22] Frances Winwar (Grebanier) notes that Wilde's mantels were piled high with blue china after the fashion established by Rossetti,[23] and Wilde's declaration, "Oh, would that I could live up to my blue china!" had probably become general knowledge.[24] A few more glosses may be of use. "Kool'em" in line 4 is probably a backwards formation meaning "look at them," lying askew on "our old meogginee," mahogany, probably the dining table (but also, perhaps not just coincidentally, the name of a drink made with brandy and water). At any rate, the wife argues that her collection is better than "a pot'n' a screw" (a flagon of liquor and a bottle of wine), and she refuses to part with it. The allusion to "flue" in line 10 may not mean to discard, but to sell, perhaps illegally. The "flue-game," according to Eric Partridge's *Dictionary of the Underworld*, was a "small-scale confidence trick involving the changing and palming of money." Finally, the phrase in the refrain, "utterly too-too," may refer to a popular song of the era by Robert Coote satirizing Wilde and the esthetes, entitled "Quite Too Utterly Utter."[25]

Of a considerably different nature is John Davidson's villanelle from *In a Music Hall* (1891), generally regarded as the first serious villanelle in English, and probably deserving of recognition as the first one written in contemporary, standard idiom. The meter is anapestic trimeter, usually with one or two unstressed syllables omitted.

> On her hand she leans her head
>   By the banks of the busy Clyde;
> Our two little boys are in bed.
>
> The pitiful tears are shed;
>   She has nobody by her side;
> On her hand she leans her head.
>
> I should be working; instead
>   I dream of my sorrowful bride,
> And our two little boys in bed.
>
> Were it well if we four were dead?
>   The grave at least is wide.
> On her hand she leans her head.
>
> She stares at the embers red;
>   She dashes the tears aside,
> And kisses our boys in bed.
>
> "God, give us our daily bread;
>   Nothing we ask beside."
> On her hand she leans her head;
> Our two little boys are in bed.[26]

Although Davidson begins with heavily alliterated lines, he does not allow the device to control the poem. And although he finds it necessary to use an inversion to achieve the rhyme in line 13, the rhymes are generally not forced, and line 7 is skillfully enjambed. Most important, from a technical standpoint, is Davidson's willingness, despite the advice of various manuals of versification, to admit slight variations in the refrain at lines 9 and 15. He is among the few early writers of the villanelle in English to follow Gosse's lead in this respect. Fortunately, he does not join the ranks of those, including Gosse, who laced their poems with poetic diction, epithets, and archaisms. The jobless husband and father, who is the speaker, is sitting in the music hall, powerless to sustain his family. All he can do is daydream of his wretched wife and speculate as to whether death would be preferable. Unlike so many other villanelles, therefore, Davidson's has a perceptible dramatic core. There is an interior drama—the one in the speaker's mind—and there is a sort of tension building toward a crisis. The speaker in these poems seems never to be very far from Davidson himself, who eventually committed suicide.

The five villanelles written by Ernest Dowson, a principal member of the Rhymers' Club, along with Davidson, Lionel Johnson, and Arthur Symons, are more indicative of the form in its early stages of development among poets writing in English. Like Henley and Lang, he has one poem devoted to the villanelle itself, "Villanelle of His Lady's Treasures" (1893).

> I took her dainty eyes, as well
>   As silken tendrils of her hair:
> And so I made a Villanelle!
>
> I took her voice, a silver bell,
>   As clear as song, as soft as prayer;
> I took her dainty eyes as well.
>
> It may be, said I, who can tell,
>   These things shall be my less despair?
> And so I made a Villanelle!
>
> I took her whiteness virginal
>   And from her cheeks two roses rare:
> I took her dainty eyes as well.
>
> I said: "It may be possible
>   Her image from my heart to tear!"
> And so I made a Villanelle!
>
> I stole her laugh, most musical:
>   I wrought it in with artful care;
> I took her dainty eyes as well;
> And so I made a Villanelle.[27]

The reference to "dainty eyes" in his controlling metaphor identifies Dowson as a poet sympathetic to Gosse's views of the limited range of the form. Even the music of the villanelle is trivialized to that of the tinkling bell (not brass, but silver). Technically, one might note the firm end-stoppage at the second line of each stanza. This makes variation in the meaning of the refrain lines through different contexts nearly impossible to achieve, since the refrain does not actually become part of the new context provided by the first two lines of the tercet. Subtlety and spontaneity are also lost. Dowson does, however, relax somewhat the standards of rhyme, permitting slant or near rhyme with virginal/possible/musical/opposite well/Villanelle.

Rather than examine any of Dowson's less effective efforts closely, we might instead look at his "Villanelle of Acheron" (1890) which, with the "Villanelle of Marguerites" (1894), represents some attempt to avoid the tendency of the form to dissolve into cliché and banality, though not without archaisms.

> By the pale marge of Acheron,
>   Methinks we shall pass restfully,
> Beyond the scope of any sun.
>
> There all men hie them one by one,
>   Far from the stress of earth and sea,
> By the pale marge of Acheron.
>
> 'Tis well when life and love is done,
>   'Tis very well at last to be,
> Beyond the scope of any sun.
>
> No busy voices there shall stun
>   Our ears: the stream flows silently
> By the pale marge of Acheron.
>
> There is the crown of labour won,
>   The sleep of immortality,
> Beyond the scope of any sun.
>
> Life, of thy gifts I will have none,
>   My queen is that Persephone,
> By the pale marge of Acheron,
>   Beyond the scope of any sun. (pp. 131–32)

As with other poets of the era, Dowson is aided by the classical context, and in fact this poem may owe something to the Theocritan villanelles of Dobson, Wilde, and Lang.

In a number of Dowson's villanelles, as in those of other poets who have attempted the form, both early and late, there is a tendency for the second line of the concluding couplet to break apart from the first. For example, in his "Villanelle of Sunset" (1892) he concludes: "Come hither, Child! and rest;/Behold the weary West!" (p. 8), and "Villanelle of Marguerites" ends: "*A little, passionately, not at all!*"/And what care we how many petals fall!" (p. 18). "Villanelle of the Poet's Road" (1895) concludes: "Wine and Women and song?/Yet is day over long" (p. 130). These couplets are not uniformly strained, but the couplet at which Dowson arrives in "Villanelle of Acheron" is certainly superior to all of them. It reads as a compound prepositional phrase, the whole of which evolves naturally from the first two lines of the quatrain as a coherent unit of thought.

Dowson also achieves in the "Villanelle of Acheron" at least one rather impressive line, and that is the first line of the poem. The aural qualities of "marge" and "Acheron" are partly responsible for the effect of this line. "Pale" is much more powerful, with its connotation of unnatural colorlessness, than would be the more obviously emotional "dark," which would probably have overtaxed the taste for assonance. The rhythm of this line is also appealing, especially playing against the very regular iambic tetrameter of the other refrain line. I scan it as follows (allowing secondary stress to the final syllable): "By the pále márge of Ácherón." Unlike his other villanelles, this one is unmarred by excessive, hard end-punctuation in the initial two lines of the stanzas. In his other villanelles colons, semicolons, question marks, and exclamation points cause frequent interruptions of the lyrical flow, often, as I have shown, breaking the statement of the stanza away from the refrain line. In the "Villanelle of Acheron" the comma predominates, and the enjambment in the fourth stanza is especially effective.

The shortcomings of Dowson's villanelle are sufficiently obvious not to need rehearsal, but they are representative of the snares which often trapped even the best poets of the age. The lure of the archaism ("methinks" being only the most obvious example) was to plague poetry for another half generation, even while poets like Pound, Eliot, and Williams were weeding it. For some reason, too, the villanelle seems to have been exceptionally vulnerable to the cliché, of which the fifth tercet provides all too apt an example. Finally, there remains that apparent inclination to limit the villanelle to those milder strains of nostalgia which offer only a low-key pathos even when dealing with the contemplation of death. This weakness applies even to Davidson's more consciously "naturalistic" villanelle discussed above.

The adoption of the villanelle by English poets of the latter half of the nineteenth century is particularly surprising, because no significant body of villanelles existed in French poetry and no major French poet had written one. That is, there was not for the villanelle such a continental reputation as there was for the sonnet, the ballade, or terza rima. Moreover, one might argue that the thematic limitations of the first English villanelles result primarily from imitation of the known French examples, notably those of Passerat, Banville, and Boulmier. Late Victorian English poets had experimented with rhythm in the form, and they had, in the direction of convention, fixed the number of stanzas at six (nineteenth-century French poets commonly departed from Passerat's model in that respect). Finally, although the villanelle had been a receptacle for the sometimes "decadent" sentiments of the age, poets like Henley and Davidson had shown that the form allowed for some thematic flexibility, both comic and serious.

The First American Villanelles

By the 1890's the villanelle was being included in texts concerning English versification, though sometimes reluctantly. As early as 1885 Francis B. Gummere alluded to Gosse's essay in his *Handbook of Poetics* (Boston: Ginn), pp. 55, 241–42. James C. Parsons includes a description and quotes villanelles by Henley and Gosse in his *English Versification* (Boston: Sibley, 1891), pp. 125ff. Robert F. Brewer lists the villanelle in a chapter entitled "Poetic Trifles" in his *Orthometry* (New York: Putnam, 1893). As these citations suggest, the villanelle had crossed the Atlantic.

The first villanelle by a "known" or an "established" American poet, though his claim is not generally acknowledged (perhaps justly), is James Whitcomb Riley's "The Best is Good Enough," originally published in 1883. Riley's villanelle harbors most of the shortcomings of those by English poets of the era when it comes to matters of technique, but the language, marked with midwestern colloquialism, is preferable to the stilted archaism of Gosse and his followers.

> I quarrel not with Destiny,
> But make the best of everything—
> The best is good enough for me.
>
> Leave Discontent alone, and she
> Will shut her mouth and let *you* sing.
> I quarrel not with Destiny.
>
> I take some things, or let 'em be—
> Good gold has always got the ring;
> The best is good enough for me.
>
> Since Fate insists on secrecy,

> I have no arguments to bring —
> I quarrel not with Destiny.
>
> The fellow that goes "haw" for "gee"
> Will find he hasn't got full swing.
> The best is good enough for me.
>
> One only knows our needs, and He
> Does all of the distributing.
> I quarrel not with Destiny:
> The best is good enough for me.[28]

If the dialect were more prevalent and the statement were less sanctimonious, this villanelle might rival Henley's "Now Ain't They Utterly Too-Too" for comic effect. As it is, Riley's "let 'em be" rings out of harmony with the stiff "I quarrel not," and the flurry of abstractions — destiny, the best, discontent, fate — conflicts with the occasionally effective figurative language, as in the fifth tercet. As with other practitioners of the form, Riley cannot integrate the refrain lines with the other lines of his tercets (note the punctuation of the various second lines), though his enjambment shows a genuine concern for sustaining the flow between lines. His concluding couplet has some appeal, perhaps in a jingoistic sort of way that seems appropriate for the times.

Edwin Arlington Robinson's *Children of the Night* (1897) includes two villanelles which are quite different in tone from those of Riley or of the English poets of the era. Robinson was probably introduced to the form through the influential hometown physician, Alanson Tucker Schumann, or by his high school teacher, Caroline Swan, or he may have encountered it during his stay at Harvard, where his first villanelle was published.[29] "Villanelle of Change" (first published in the *Harvard Advocate* in 1891) and "The House on the Hill" (first published in *The Globe* in 1894) are poems haunted by the past. There is some element of the classicist's nostalgia in the "Villanelle of Change," in which the battleground at Marathon is a commemorative not only of the Persian defeat, but also of the decline of Hellenic culture:

> The suns of Hellas have all shone,
>   The first has fallen to the last: —
> Since Persia fell at Marathon,
> Long centuries have come and gone.[30]

If the Persians fell at Marathon, so too did the glorious but also decadent Greeks. The poem has moments of excellence, as in the implied metaphor of the second line: "The yellow years have gathered fast." But like most writers of the villanelle, Robinson cannot avoid some awk-ward syntactic inversion, as in line 8: " . . . when Helicon/Trembled and swayed with rapture vast." Perhaps what most distinguishes this villanelle, and the more renowned "The House on the Hill," is its free-dom from archaisms. One searches in vain, happily, for the baggage of wouldst/methinks/thou bad'st/'tis that burdens so many of the English villanelles of the period.

"The House on the Hill" has attracted more attention than any other early villanelle written in English. Although there have been some discordant notes, such as William Peterfield Trent's rebuke for the poem's "impressionistic effect" (in the *Sewanee Review* for April 1897), most early reviewers and subsequent commentators have agreed with Joyce Kilmer who, in the *New York Times Review of Books* for September 8, 1912, hailed the "striking simplicity" of the poem, "so different in spirit from the traditional villanelle that its form is at first scarcely recognized."[31]

> They are all gone away,
>   The House is shut and still,
> There is nothing more to say.
>
> Through broken walls and gray
>   The winds blow bleak and shrill.
> They are all gone away.
>
> Nor is there one to-day
>   To speak them good or ill:
> There is nothing more to say.
>
> Why is it then we stray
>   Around the sunken sill?
> They are all gone away,
>
> And our poor fancy-play
>   For them is wasted skill:
> There is nothing more to say.
>
> There is ruin and decay
>   In the House on the Hill:
> They are all gone away,
> There is nothing more to say. (pp. 81–82)

Theodore Roosevelt, in his review of *Children of the Night* (*Outlook*, August 12, 1905), quotes the poem and observes that "Whoever has lived in country America knows the gray, empty houses from which life has gone" (Cary, p. 170). The poem soon became a popular anthology piece, selected by Edwin Markham for his *Book of Poetry*, II (1926) and by Mark Van Doren for *American Poets 1630-1930* (1933).

In his account of the composition of "The House on the Hill," recorded in a letter to Harry DeForest Smith dated 25 February 1894, Robinson explains that he tried the villanelle in part as an exercise to write himself out of a bad mood during an excessively cold and bleak winter. He describes the poem as "a little mystical perhaps and . . . an attempt to show the poetry of the commonplace."[32] He confesses a fascination for the "old French forms" and claims to have turned out this villanelle in just twenty minutes. In another letter to Smith, in April of the same year, Robinson indicates his preference "for the suggestiveness of these artificial forms — that is, when they treat of something besides bride-roses and ball-rooms" (p. 146). It is with poems like "The House on the Hill" and Davidson's "On Her Hand She Leans Her Head" that the villanelle begins to escape, in English and American poetry, from the confines of *jeu d'esprit* and *vers de société*. In some ways, this transition returns the villanelle to the state it was in during the sixteenth century when, if it was not quite a form of "popular" poetry, it was at least written in the language of "a man speaking to men."

Robinson altered considerably the second and third tercets of "The House on the Hill" after his first version was published. The original stanzas were as follows:

> Malign them as we may,
>   We cannot do them ill:
> They are all gone away.
>
> Are we more fit than they
>   To meet the Master's will? —
> There is nothing more to say. (*Letters*, p. 132)

In this early version the implicit autobiographical reference may seem even more marked than in the final version. The antagonism between "we" and "they" is emphasized, and the speaker is more willing to moralize. Robinson was firm, however, in denying that any specific reference was intended in the poem.[33] As revised, the poem stresses the bareness of the scene and the irretrievability of the past, yet also the inevitability of human fascination with it. The concern of this poem with the impossibility of ever really knowing the truth, beyond a few facts, and in this case a very few facts, is a basic theme in Robinson's poetry. It is, for example, the central theme of the admired "Richard

Cory." By rendering the "we" of the poem not maligners, but speakers of neither good nor evil who simply allow their imaginations to run loose, Robinson asserts, in his revised version of the poem, the distance between people which he himself felt all his life.

Robinson's and Davidson's modernization of the language (in both diction and syntax), subject matter, and thematic or conceptual nature of the villanelle did not have immediate influence on other writers of the form in England and the United States. Helen Louise Cohen's anthology of thirty-five villanelles in *Lyric Forms from France* (New York: Harcourt, 1922) includes the work of several minor poets, British and American, whose works and reputations have faded into near oblivion: John Payne, Clinton Scollard, Franklin P. Adams, Edith M. Thomas. There are numerous curiosities and occasional familiar names to be encountered among the villanelles of the first decades of the twentieth century. There is, for example, Louis Untermeyer's "Lugubrious Villanelle of Platitudes" written in iambic heptameter, good, clumsy fourteeners, quite appropriate to the comic effect. There is a silly villanelle on how easy it is to write villanelles by the scholar, W. W. Skeat, and there is (an earlier poem) Cotsford Dick's attempt to compose a villanelle and imitate Anglo-Saxon alliterative verse simultaneously, "A Vacation Villanelle" (1886). There are the villanelles of Walter Adolphe Roberts, a black poet whose poems, like "Villanelle of the Living Pan," show no trace of Langston Hughes and the Harlem Renaissance.

Among the best known early twentieth-century villanelles are Ezra Pound's irregular "Villanelle: The Psychological Hour," which first appeared in *Poetry*, VIII (December 1915) and James Joyce's "Are You Not Weary of Ardent Ways," the fixed-form villanelle that Stephen Daedalus composes for his sweetheart of ten years past in *A Portrait of the Artist as a Young Man* (1916). Helen Cohen's book, however, marks a convenient stopping place for a survey of the development of the fixed-form villanelle in English and American poetry. A generation of poets, in England stretching from the latter years of Victoria through the reign of Edward VII and into that of George V, had lived through the last strains of post-Romanticism. World War I and the Jazz Age with its "lost generations" would alter the character of Western poetry and culture in such a way that the villanelle, as Gosse and Dowson and Dobson and Wilde conceived it, could be written only by those versifiers who find all ages reducible to posies. Pound's irregular form villanelle represents one aspect of things to come, the repudiation of traditional forms, or at least their radical modification. The villanelles of William Empson, one of which was first published in 1928, and those of W. H. Auden, which date from 1940, are distinctively "modern" poems and belong, like the great villanelles of Dylan Thomas and Theodore Roethke, to another stage in the development of the form.

◆

5.
From Ezra Pound to Mid-Century:
The Form in a Major Key

*I*n his preface to Lionel Johnson's poems, Ezra Pound concedes that one ought not to "condemn the 'stanza poem' categorically" and suggests that "The villanelle, even, can at its best achieve the closest intensity, I mean when, as with Dowson, the refrains are an emotional fact, which the intellect, in the various gyrations of the poem, tries in vain and in vain to escape."[1] That Pound was not himself interested in writing a typical villanelle can be verified by his "Villanelle: The Psychological Hour," first published in *Poetry* in 1915, the year that he wrote the preface to Johnson's poems. K. K. Ruthven points out that while Pound knew of the fixed-form villanelle, this poem is "a villanelle in name only."[2]

I

I had over-prepared the event,
  that much was ominous.
With middle-ageing care
  I had laid out just the right books.
I had almost turned down the pages.

  Beauty is so rare a thing.
  So few drink of my fountain.

So much barren regret,
So many hours wasted!
And now I watch, from the window,
  the rain, the wandering buses.
"Their little cosmos is shaken"—
  the air is alive with the fact.
In their parts of the city
  they are played on by diverse forces.
How do I know?

O, I know well enough.
For them there is something afoot.
   As for me;
I had over-prepared the event—

   Beauty is so rare a thing
   So few drink of my fountain.

Two friends: a breath of the forest . . .
Friends? Are people less friends
   because one has just, at last, found them?
Twice they promised to come.

   "Between the night and the morning?"
   Beauty would drink of my mind.

Youth would awhile forget
   my youth is gone from me.

II

("Speak up! You have danced so stiffly?
   Someone admired your works,
   And said so frankly
   "Did you talk like a fool,
   The first night?
   The second evening?"
But they promised again:
   'To-morrow at tea-time.' ")

III

Now the third day is here—
   no word from either;
No word from her nor him,
Only another man's note:
   "Dear Pound, I am leaving England."[3]

Although there is very little in the above that is villanelle-like, I would like to account for the extent to which Pound deals with the conventions of the villanelle in this poem. If one were to take the italicized refrain lines in the first stanza as a unit in tercet form, one would have the start to a conventional villanelle:

   Beauty is so rare a thing.
   So few drink of my fountain.
   "Between the night and morning?"

Did Pound, perhaps, begin with these three rather provocative seven-syllable lines rhyming, as the conventional villanelle tercet, *aba*? Of course, any such assumption would be strictly in the realm of hypothesis, but surely the title of the poem and the particular stress on the lines invite such speculation.

Beyond the possibility of concealed form, however, "The Psychological Hour" is a villanelle in another sense. As Pound observed, the important thing is that the refrain constitute an "emotional fact" and that the remainder of the poem be a vain attempt to "escape" by intellectual maneuvering. Certainly that is what occurs in this villanelle. The aging speaker, aware of the rarity and evanescence of beauty, finds himself isolated, and the conclusion he draws is not "obvious" but "ominous." The first section concludes with a somewhat fanciful gyration of the intellect. Instead of his mind drinking from the fountain of beauty, beauty would drink of his mind, and youth, should those friends appear, would "forget" his age. The rhetorical devices in this section are fairly extensive. There are the refrain lines, some anaphora, a brief apostrophe, some metaphoric play ("a breath of the forest . . . "), schematic repetition in the form of epanalepsis ("Friends? Are people less friends"), and at least one example of ploce or antanaclasis ("Youth would awhile forget/my youth is gone from me.").

In the parenthetical second section of the poem, a colloquy which occurs on the second day, the speaker identifies himself as a writer apprehensive over the approval of those who "drink at his fountain." This section is considerably shorter and less meandering than the first, but the emotional pitch is higher. There are questions and self-criticism ("Did you talk like a fool . . . "). One might say that the emotional facts are becoming more difficult to escape.

In the terse third section, corresponding to the third day, the voice is flat and the statement strictly denotative. The writer reveals his actual identity, for he is indeed trapped: it is Pound himself. No amount of intellectual gyration can save the speaker who, in being named, loses any hope of psychological "escape."

Almost totally opposite Pound's effort to capture the "sense" or the "feeling" of the villanelle, in their rigidity of form, are William Empson's three villanelles published between 1928 and 1940. Perhaps no other writer of the form, early or modern, is more severe in his insistence upon end-stopping lines. Empson's villanelles all begin with a tercet in which each line terminates in a period. Of fifty-four lines that could be enjambed in his three villanelles, Empson enjambs only eight. He never varies the refrain lines in the slightest, and each poem runs the conventional nineteen lines. The effect, of course, is of the stiffest formality.

But this stiffness also affects the syntax of the poem, as in the fourth stanza of "Villanelle," where the syntactic awkwardness is occasioned by various inversions:

> How safe I felt, whom memory assures,
> Rich that your grace safely by heart I knew.
> It is the pain, it is the pain, endures.[4]

As Philip and Averil Gardner have observed, Empson's "pentameters and heavy monosyllables" amount to a sort of repudiation of the general grace and nostalgia in the villanelles of Austin Dobson, William Dowson, and Oscar Wilde.[5] Consider, too, the opening tercet of "Missing Dates," first published in 1937:

> Slowly the poison the whole blood stream fills.
> It is not the effort nor the failure tires.
> The waste remains, the waste remains and kills. (p. 62)

One might argue, of course, that the stiffness of form is well suited to the sombre content. These lines could hardly differ more in form or content from the opening tercets of a generation earlier:

> A voice in the scented night, —
>   A step where the rose-trees blow, —
> O Love, and O Love's delight!

> (Austin Dobson, "Villanelle at Verone")[6]

> I took her dainty eyes, as well
>   As silken tendrils of her hair:
> And so I made a Villanelle!

> (Ernest Dowson, "Villanelle of His Lady's Treasures")[7]

W. H. Auden's "If I Could Tell You" (1940), originally entitled "But I Can't," is conventional in form until the last stanza, in which he converts the declarative first refrain line to a question.

> Time will say nothing but I told you so,
> Time only knows the price we have to pay;
> If I could tell you I would let you know.

> If we should weep when clowns put on their show,
> If we should stumble when musicians play,
> Time will say nothing but I told you so.

> There are no fortunes to be told, although,
> Because I love you more than I can say,
> If I could tell you I would let you know.

The winds must come from somewhere when they blow,
There must be reasons why the leaves decay;
Time will say nothing but I told you so.

Perhaps the roses really want to grow,
The vision seriously intends to stay;
If I could tell you I would let you know.

Suppose the lions all get up and go,
And all the brooks and soldiers run away;
Will Time say nothing but I told you so?
If I could tell you I would let you know.[8]

Perhaps this poem provides some evidence of Pound's observation that the refrain lines provide "emotional fact," against which the other lines gyrate intellectually. But as one critic has noted, the poem "is not, in places, far removed from the kind of sentiment found in the popular commercial song."[9] That comment is unintentionally reminiscent of the quasipopular origins of the form in Italian song and verse. There is, however, a sort of ease, a "patness," to this poem, to which detractors of the form legitimately object. In modern and contemporary poetry, the rift between popular verse and "sophisticated" poetry has widened, perhaps irrevocably.

Of greater interest is Auden's love poem, "Alone" (originally, "Are You There?"), which was also written in 1940. Unlike Empson's villanelles, and others of his own ("If I Could Tell You," above, and "Miranda," part of *The Sea and the Mirror*), the lines in this poem are very relaxed. Of the eighteen lines that could be enjambed, eight are. Moreover, the refrain lines are altered considerably throughout, except for the last words.

Each lover has a theory of his own
About the difference between the ache
Of being with his love, and being alone:

Why what, when dreaming, is dear flesh and bone
That really stirs the senses, when awake,
Appears a simulacrum of his own.

Narcissus disbelieves in the unknown;
He cannot join his image in the lake
So long as he assumes he is alone.

The child, the waterfall, the fire, the stone,
Are always up to mischief, though, and take

The universe for granted as their own.

The elderly, like Proust, are always prone
To think of love as a subjective fake;
The more they love, the more they feel alone.

Whatever view we hold, it must be shown
Why every lover has a wish to make
Some other kind of otherness his own:
Perhaps, in fact, we never are alone.[10]

The result of changing the refrain lines throughout the poem is, among
other things, the loss of tension between emotional fact and intellectual
gyration. The second stanza already implies the resolution, that "we
never are alone," and throughout Auden leaves hints of it. Narcissus
"*assumes* he is alone"; the elderly "*feel* alone." The child, like other natural phenomena, takes "for granted" his identity and unity with the universe. The lover's "wish to make/Some other kind of otherness his own"
amounts to an intuitive or tacit recognition that the "flesh and bone"
dream is identical in a way with the mere image (simulacrum) experi-
enced in waking. Put another way, since the "ache" of being with the
beloved is like that of being apart, and since waking reality is no more
actual than dreamed reality, we are never alone.

Probably spurred by the work of Empson and Auden, the villanelle "came of age" in the 1950's. Between 1951 and 1957 conventional, fixed-form villanelles were written or published by several major
poets, including Dylan Thomas, Sylvia Plath, Theodore Roethke, and
Richard Eberhart. The efforts of these poets have made the form accessible to the contemporaries, poets of the 1960's through the 1980's, most
of whom proceed from Thomas, Plath, or Roethke, and very few of
whom appear to be aware of the long history and development of the
form.

Dylan Thomas's "Do Not Go Gentle into that Good Night, the
epigraph to this book, which commemorates his father's approaching
death, exhorts the aged to be courageous, and celebrates the paradox of
the human condition, has become the acknowledged masterpiece of the
form. The poem has been extensively examined and elaborately praised.
Louise Baughan Murdy, who analyzes the aural qualities of the poem,
describes it as "a poem of great force, beauty, and tenderness, in which
sound and sense are exquisitely blended."[11] Observing that Thomas has
"found the inevitable form for his purposes," William York Tindall finds
the poem "one of the most moving tributes of son to father in all

literature."[12] Although his response shows some inconsistency in the eight years separating his books on Thomas, David Holbrook concludes that the poem records a moment of "great poignancy" and that despite some "cumbersome" conceits, "there is a certain deeply moving quality about its attempts to transcend the conventional elegiac."[13] Holbrook finds the poem "incantatory" and "ritualistic," a natural by-product, perhaps of the villanelle's reiterative nature.

Much of the commentary on "Do Not Go Gentle" is biographical, that of Holbrook being perhaps the most extensive and provocative. "The main energy of the poem," Holbrook argues, "is directed at this failure of the father to achieve greatness."[14] But while the reference of the poem to Thomas's father is undeniable, other themes register on the reader more immediately and with at least equal force. Old men, even more than the wise or the good, the wild or the grave, should lash out against death, because more than others they have occupied their time with mere living. Moreover, as Sir Thomas Browne remarked, "the long habit of living indisposeth us for dying." As much as the poem is about Thomas's father, it never ceases to be about the human condition in general, with its frustrated ambitions and its futile pursuit of such wisdom or action that might counter the prospect of death. This is "heroism" in the sense that Ernest Becker defines it in *The Denial of Death*: "heroism is first and foremost a reflex of the terror of death."[15]

Thomas uses the villanelle form masterfully. The gravity of subject obviously requires the decasyllabic line, as opposed to the "lighter" octosyllabic line, and the form itself is such that paradoxes and antitheses, so central to Thomas's poetic vision, can be worked out in contiguous stanzas at some extent, and yet with considerable pointedness: wise man/dark/words, as a unit of concept and image, is countered by good men/bright/deeds; wild men/sang/sun/grieve strains against grave men/see/meteors/gay. The poem begins with a demand apparently aimed at old people. This might amount to Pound's "emotional fact." The next four tercets provide a sort of categorical analysis against which the refrains incessantly urge, "Do not go gentle" and "Rage." After rereading the poem, one tends to forget the genuine surprise of the last stanza, in which the immediate object of Thomas's imperative is revealed as his father. Prior to this revelation, there has been no appearance of a first person voice, and the reader has been encouraged to assume that the imperatives of the first stanza and the refrains are aimed at man in general rather than any particular person. The introduction into the last section of the poet's own voice provides a special intensity and intimacy, which accounts for much of the poem's impact.

After "Do Not Go Gentle," the most influential villanelle for contemporary poets has been Theodore Roethke's "The Waking," also an epigraph to this book, the title poem of his 1953 volume. Karl Malkoff calls the poem "one of Roethke's most successful unions of form and content."[16] Perhaps even more than Thomas, Roethke employs paradox in his villanelle, and like Thomas, he chooses the decasyllabic line, departing from strict adherence to the conventions only in the refrain line of the penultimate stanza. The similarities between the poems, however, are really rather slight. The first person is dominant throughout Roethke's poem, and there is not that close parallel relationship in idea and image from stanza to stanza that figures in Thomas's villanelle.

The relationship between the first two tercets of "The Waking" is fairly close, from "feel my fate" and "learn by going" to "think by feeling" and "know." But the connection between the second and third tercets is not so clear. The "you" introduced in the first line of the tercet is never really accounted for, and there is no apparent conceptual or imagistic link between the stanzas. Rather, Roethke's poem appears to move by leaps, at least after the second stanza. What connection exists among the intriguing three lines of the fourth stanza? They seem almost disembodied. There is a question, which provides whatever coherence might be said to exist among the second, third, and fourth tercets, but the line after the question — who can tell us how "Light takes the Tree'? — turns to the "lowly worm" climbing the "winding stair." The latter metaphor might derive from Bacon's "Of Great Place": "All rising to great place is by a winding stair." It also appears in George Herbert's poetry, or it might be drawn from one of Yeats's several winding stairways. The speaker, at any rate, would seem to be similar in some ways to the "lowly worm," for the refrain reminds us that he also proceeds slowly.

The third stanza, in which "Great Nature" is evoked, reminds us of the words capitalized in the two previous stanzas, "Ground" and "Tree." That which roots the speaker to material reality is stressed. The ascent is completed in this tercet, in which the implied listener is advised, apparently in the face of death, since "Great Nature has another thing to do" to us, not for us, to "take the lively air." At this point, the refrain line takes an important shift in reference. The "I" is left out and the listener is addressed directly. The elided syllables are replaced with the parenthetical adverb "lovely," which may be read variously as "you lovely person" Or "in a lovely fashion." The play of "lively" and "lovely" is a sort of musical bonus.

In the concluding stanza the voice appears to be most painfully that of Roethke himself, enervated, alcoholic, neurotic: "This shaking keeps me steady." The paradox is ironic—whether bitterly or playfully it is hard to tell, but the voice on the recordings suggests the former. The paradoxes of the next line, however, are healing: "What falls away is always. And is near." Malkoff considers the poem a "stoic" acceptance of the "natural cycle."[17] Roethke's following of Empson's closely end-stopped lines contributes to the sense of stern self-control, the necessity of proceeding with caution, and the realization that education is a continuous experience. Particularly in the last stanza, Roethke uses tight, clipped (one is tempted to say "Senecan") syntax in order to stress the imposition of personal control, despite the dictates of fortune or fate which will tell him where he has to go.

> This shaking keeps me steady. I should know.
> What falls away is always. And is near.
> I wake to sleep, and take my waking slow.
> I learn by going where I have to go.[18]

Quite unlike "The Waking" in tone and in use of the villanelle form is "The Right Thing," which appears in Roethke's last volume, *The Far Field* (1964). Jenijoy La Belle finds the source of the poem in the *beatus ille* tradition of Ben Jonson's verse epistles.[19] Malkoff sees in the poem the achievement of "unity of being" and the acceptance of "an eternal purpose behind the apparent flux of reality."[20]

> Let others probe the mystery if they can.
> Time-harried prisoners of *Shall* and *Will*—
> The right thing happens to the happy man.
>
> The bird flies out, the bird flies back again;
> The hill becomes the valley, and is still;
> Let others delve that mystery if they can.
>
> God bless the roots!—Body and soul are one!
> The small becomes the great, the great the small;
> The right thing happens to the happy man.
>
> Child of the dark, he can out leap the sun,
> His being single, and that being all:
> The right thing happens to the happy man.

Or he sits still, a solid figure when
The self-destructive shake the common wall;
Takes to himself what mystery he can,

And, praising change as the slow night comes on,
Wills what he would, surrendering his will
Till mystery is no more: No more he can.
The right thing happens to the happy man.[21]

Whereas periods or question marks end eleven of the nineteen lines in
"The Waking," only eight lines are so fully end-stopped in "The Right
Thing." Neither poem offers much in the way of enjambed lines, and
the initial two lines of the tercets tend to be somewhat isolated from the
refrain line in Roethke's villanelles, but the latter poem is somewhat
looser than "The Waking," involving, in fact, a syntactic continuation
between the fifth and sixth stanzas.

Whereas "The Waking" involves persistent questioning of the paradoxes of the human condition and intense concentration on the self
(the word "I" appears fourteen times in the poem), "The Right Thing"
is casual in every way: "Let others probe the mystery if they can." One
measure of the casual tone is Roethke's surrender of the harried first
person speaker in favor of the more neutral, more universal third person. Another measure of the ease of this poem is the relaxation of caesura. Six lines in "The Waking" are broken by medial punctuation (semicolons, periods) sufficient to cause a considerable interruption of rhythm.
This sort of caesura occurs only twice in "The Right Thing." (I omit
commas from consideration in both poems.) Moreover, although "the
Waking" involves some departures from form (some slant- and eye-
rhymes; two alterations of the second refrain line, the most important
of which was noted above), Roethke experiments with the form quite
freely in "The Right Thing." The can/man (A^1/A^2) rhymes are
again/one/sun/when/on—not one true rhyme in the lot. The *b* rhyme
alternates between -ill and -all. More importantly, the second refrain
line varies throughout, and the alternation of refrain lines is disrupted
at the fourth stanza. What happens, in effect, is that the "mystery" of
life is a result of its changeableness, but the response of "the happy
man," a "solid figure," remains fixed, permanent in the face of flux.

Of the several villanelles which Sylvia Plath apparently wrote as
exercises, sometimes during class, only her "favorite," "Mad Girl's Love
Song," written in 1951 when she was about nineteen, has been published.[22]

I shut my eyes and all the world drops dead;
I lift my lids and all is born again.
(I think I made you up inside my head.)

The stars go waltzing out in blue and red,
And arbitrary blackness gallops in:
I shut my eyes and all the world drops dead.

I dreamed that you bewitched me into bed
And sung me moon-struck, kissed me quite insane.
(I think I made you up inside my head.)

God topples from the sky, hell's fires fade:
Exit Seraphim and Satan's men:
I shut my eyes and all the world drops dead.

I fancied you'd return the way you said,
But I grow old and I forget your name.
(I think I made you up inside my head.)

I should have loved a thunderbird instead;
At least when spring comes they roar back again.
I shut my eyes and all the world drops dead.
(I think I made you up inside my head.)[23]

Edward Butscher describes the refrain lines as a statement of "the unavoidable, poetically banal truths of the child moving from innocence into adult reality with his awesome ego intact," but also, in the context of the poet's biography, "madness refined to purest self."[24] In the mind of the rejected girl, the loss of the beloved is akin to the loss of the world; or, more accurately, there is no distinction between the losses. She has lost her personal grasp of reality. The poem, therefore, is a statement of insanity and apocalypse. There can be no real "answer" to the dilemma, since the agony is already upon her. All she can do is rave: "I should have loved a thunderbird instead." The mythical Indian bringer of rain and thunder, though suitably ominous in its power, would at least return. The appearance of the thunderbird may seem curious in the last section of a poem which has offered no suggestion of Indian lore, but throughout, the poem has drawn upon celestial images: the stars waltz in stanza two (the harmonious dance of love yielding to chaotic blackness, which gallops); the speaker is "moon-struck" in stanza three; "God topples from the sky" in stanza four. The thunderbird is a celestial power, essentially male, which is related to fertility rites. It provides an appropriate metaphoric conclusion to the poem.

Like Plath's villanelle, Richard Eberhart's draws more on antithesis than on paradox, but it is considerably more reflective or meditative in tone than the villanelles that "take after" Thomas. The voice is closer to that of Auden.

Christ is walking in your blood today,
His gentle tread you cannot hear nor see.
He tramples down your militant wish to slay.

The whelped deaths you dealt in your war's day
Arise howling, they will never make you free.
Christ is walking in your blood today.

You did it easily in the heat of the fray.
You did not know what you could do, could be.
He tramples down the massive wish to slay.

You are the front and fore of passion's play,
Of deepest knowledge you have lost the key.
Christ is walking in your blood today.

To kill is one, is not the essential way
Of action, which you then could not foresee.
He will wash the welling blood. Not slay.

A child becomes a man who learns to pray,
A child-like silence on a moveless sea.
Redeemed you may be of the will to slay.
Christ fermentative be all your blood today.[25]

Eberhart allows himself some freedom with the refrain lines, the most considerable occasion being in the fifth stanza, and he brings to the villanelle what some editors have described as his style of "cultivated and sustained awkwardness."[26] Like most writers of the villanelle, though (Auden being a notable exception), Eberhart breaks the body of the tercet away from the refrain line throughout the poem.

Unlike "the Truth" of aphorism, "The whelped deaths you dealt in your war's day" will not "make you free." In the heat of battle, men lost vision, yielded to passion. In the healing eucharist and the mystery of transubstantiation with which Eberhart concludes the poem, the man does not become a child again (in order to enter the kingdom of heaven), but the "child becomes a man" who prays "a child-like silence." The polysyllabic weight and academic wit of the phrase "Christ fermentative," however, is difficult for even the sympathetic reader to endure.

Among the five villanelles written by Weldon Kees, "one of the bitterest poets in history,"[27] who disappeared in 1955, "The Crack Moving Down the Wall" is probably the best known. Published in *The Fall of the Magicians* (1947), the poem opens with a tightly end-stopped tercet, which seems at first more regular than it is.

> The crack is moving down the wall.
> Defective plaster isn't all the cause.
> We must remain until the roof falls in.

The repeated "all" sounds (wall/all/falls) at first distract the reader's attention from the unconventional refrain rhymes (A/C rather than A^1/A^2). Perhaps not until the first line of the next tercet does the reader note the variable line length, a trademark of Kees's villanelles and less stiff or awkward than Eberhart's lines because Kees's are more regular in rhythm.

> It's mildly cheering to recall
> That every building has its little flaws.
> The crack is moving down the wall.
>
> Here in the kitchen, drinking gin,
> We can accept the damndest laws.
> We must remain until the roof falls in.
>
> And though there's no one here at all,
> One searches every room because
> The crack is moving down the wall.
>
> Repairs? But how can one begin?
> The lease has warnings buried in each clause,
> We must remain until the roof falls in.
>
> These nights one hears a creaking in the hall,
> The sort of thing that gives one pause.
> the crack is moving down the wall.
> We must remain until the roof falls in.[28]

Three of the five villanelles alternate in various ways, essentially, between octosyllabic and decasyllabic lines. The other two vary, in the case of the rather comic "A Villanelle for the Publisher Who Rejected _____'s Book," in lines of from eight to fourteen syllables, and in the more somber "No Sound Except the Beating of a Drum," from ten to twelve.

"The Crack" typifies the tone and theme of most of Kees's villanelles. Dilapidation and impending ruin are spliced with half-comical phrases and lines: "It's mildly cheering," "its little flaws," "We can accept the damndest laws," "The sort of thing that gives one pause." The result is a bizarre, sort of black-humorous effect. In "Men We Once Honored

Share a Crooked Eye" the speaker laments the inability to save the men and women destroyed by "the age," and in "No Sound" the speaker concludes:

> I think it is our hearts. Each paralyzed and numb
> With waiting. Yet what is it we are waiting for?
> No sound except the beating of a drum?
> "Time will go by," we heard. "No messages will come."[29]

Finally, in "We Had the Notion it was Dawn" the speaker is a soldier whose unit is compelled to attack despite a truce. The dawn is but "a notion," and perhaps it is connected with the conventional Hollywood notion of attacking at dawn, but it is a false dawn, and these are men "Sired in caskets, born to die at night" (one might say "benighted"). Furthermore, the speaker confesses, "We helped to choose these fields we crawl upon."[30] The use of the first person plural, the inclusive or editorial point of view, marks all four of the serious villanelles and helps create an apocalyptic atmosphere in which the speaker, like the subjects of the poems, is doomed.

Ezra Pound's radical, formless villanelle has had no direct imitators, but Lew Welch, a poet of the Beat movement in San Francisco, comes close in the first of his poems titled "Two Like Villanelles," in *Ring of Bone: Collected Poems 1950–1971*. His 17-line poem, "For all the Wet Green Girls" (61), however, comes fairly close to the conventional form in its redundancy, even though it is set up in couplets instead of tercets.[31] It is surprising to find the villanelle reaching into this most anti-formalistic and anti-academic of movements, but a very conventional one appears in Gary Snyder's recent collection of early, uncollected poems, *Left Out in the Rain* (1986), in the 1951–80 section, "Villanelle of the Wandering Lapps" (181).[32] Snyder's poem hews close to the form and is cast in iambic trimeter.

By the end of the 1950's, the villanelle had been established as an accepted form in English and American poetry. Its range had been demonstrated.[31] Despite the reiterative refrain lines, the villanelle had been proven, at least in the hands of able poets, capable of the profoundest themes, and of tones ranging from the comic to the apocalyptic, from the meditative to the enraged. Most important, however, were the achievements with the form by poets of major stature, from Pound and Auden to Thomas and Roethke. Among these poets some rather cautious experimentation with the form set the groundwork for poets of the next generation, who were to examine rigorously its potential and its limits.

6.
The Form and its Transformations in Contemporary Poetry

*A*t the same time that poets like Thomas and Roethke were widening the range of the villanelle, a number of lesser known poets were following the lead of W. H. Auden in bringing to it the special flexibility of line that has come to mark some of the best villanelles of the last thirty years. In particular, the tendency for the refrain lines to stand apart from the tercets in which they are included, even in the best villanelles, seems to have challenged a number of poets. One effect of the isolated refrain lines has often been a pair of concluding lines almost independent of one another and frequently set apart from each other by heavy terminal punctuation.

> It is the pain, it is the pain, endures.
> Poise of my hands reminded me of yours.[1]
> — Empson

> I wake to sleep, and take my waking slow.
> I learn by going where I have to go.[2]
> — Roethke

> I shut my eyes and all the world drops dead.
> (I think I made you up inside my head.)[3]
> — Plath

I do not mean to suggest that the concluding couplets above are inferior to those which have resulted from recent experimentation, but that the stiffness of the villanelle has been countered by a freer use of enjambment in the work of some poets writing in the last twenty years or so. The concluding couplets that result are quite different from these.

Joseph Langland's "Ecclesiastes," published in *Poetry Today*, III (1956), provides an example of the fluidity gained in the villanelle through the free use of enjambment, even between stanzas. (Enjambment between stanzas is not especially innovative, of course. George Herbert, among other seventeenth-century poets, experimented with cross-stanza enjambment.)

> Out of the icy storms the white hare came
> Shivering into a haven of human arms;
> It was not love but fear that made him tame.
>
> He lay in the arms of love, having no name
> but comfort to address. Shaking alarms
> Out of the icy storms, the white hare came
>
> Across the haunted meadows crackling with game.
> What evil eye pinpointed his soft charms?
> It was not love but fear. That made him tame
>
> Among the chilling hail and scattering aim.
> Helpless against the sport of ancient farms,
> Out of the icy storms the white hare came
>
> Thinking, perhaps, it leaped through icy flame,
> Thinking, with instinct, hate or trust disarms.
> It was not love. But fear that made him tame
>
> Leaped again in his heart; his flesh became
> Translated into havens. From sudden harms
> Out of the icy storms the white hare came;
> It was not love but fear that made him tame.[4]

The enjambment provides greater ease of movement in the villanelle, not only between stanzas, but also within the tercet, between the body and the refrain line. Since the poem itself involves considerable movement and action, the freer line is appropriate. New stress is also given the modifications in meaning of the refrain lines, an attribute thought essential to the form by most readers and poets.

Langland's villanelle does not conclude with a perfectly smooth, enjambed couplet, but observe the last lines of Barbara Howes' "The Triumph of Death," published in *New Poems by American Poets*, #2 (1957):

> As we approach a new plateau of love
>
> The Aspen sigh in mockery: then have
> We come this way before? Staining the air,
> Illusion forms before us like a grove
> As we approach a new plateau of love.[5]

The use of slant- and eye-rhyme, along with the freely enjambed lines, identifies this villanelle as a product of what might be considered the furthest limit of experimentation within the confines of formal convention. This is not to say that innovation and experimentation with the villanelle stops here. As I will demonstrate, the form has attracted a number of admirers who draw variously upon its conventional structure and upon its spirit. First, however, I would like to examine some villanelles written in the manner of the above, in what I will call "loose-line" form.

One of the ablest villanelles of this type is James Merrill's "The World and the Child" (1967). Both refrain lines are varied somewhat, but the second one (A^2), "Falls on the child awake and wearied of," is less variable than the first.

> Letting his wisdom be the whole of love,
> The father tiptoes out, backwards. A gleam
> Falls on the child awake and wearied of,
>
> Then, as the door clicks shut, is snuffed. The glove-
> Gray afterglow appalls him. It would seem
> That letting wisdom be the whole of love
>
> Were pastime even for the bitter grove
> Outside, whose owl's white hoot of disesteem
> Falls on the child awake and wearied of.
>
> He lies awake in pain, he does not move,
> He will not scream. Any who heard him scream
> Would let their wisdom be the whole of love.
>
> People have filled the room he lies above.
> Their talk, mild variation, chilling theme,
> Falls on the child. Awake and wearied of
>
> Mere pain, mere wisdom also, he would have
> All the world waking from its winter dream,
> Letting its wisdom be. The whole of love
> Falls on the child awake and wearied of.[6]

The simplicity of the event recounted in the poem makes it an apt subject for treatment in the villanelle form, and the added tension, though modulated when seen against the pronounced antithetical movement of such villanelles as Roethke's "The Right Thing," sustains the conceptual development. The child, closed up by his sensible father during a party, cannot accept the paradox, that wisdom and love are one. Even the natural world outside the child's room seems to agree to the paradoxical union of wisdom and love. He recognizes that if he screams, those who heard him would allow "their wisdom to be the whole of love," in that their good sense would take precedence over their love, probably in the form of punishment. In the last stanza, the child identifies "mere wisdom" with "mere pain." The banal chatter of the party downstairs, and perhaps its lovelessness ("chilling theme"), causes the child to wish that "all the world" were as awake as he from its "winter dream." Then wisdom would be seen for the "mere" thing that it is, and the "whole of love" would fall upon him.

Merrill's use of caesura in the penultimate line helps to create the antithetical conclusion: wisdom is isolated on one side of the period, and the "whole of love" opposes it. Of the eighteen lines that could be enjambed ten are, and twice this enjambment bridges stanzas. Commas end five of the remaining lines in the poem, so that a prolonged pause at the end of any line is relatively rare. Six times sentences end (with a period) in midline, creating caesura but interrupting the flow of the poem somewhat less than they would if they were placed at the ends of lines. Technically, the poem is evidence of a tendency among some contemporary poets to level punctuation. In the case of a poet like W. S. Merwin, this leveling comes to the complete rejection of punctuation, but many poets writing today have rejected the semicolon and the colon altogether and have reduced the number of commas in their poems, leaving just enough punctuation to provide coherence. The reasons for this may vary, but one may be that the poet today is extraordinarily conscious of the appearance of the poem on the page. The use of white space on the page, to represent silence, a meditative pause, or oblivion at the end of a line or stanza, makes the contemporary poet especially aware of the "weight" of a punctuation mark.[7]

Another contemporary poet who has written some villanelles in this "loose-lined" fashion is Marilyn Hacker: "I like the challenge of repetitions, seeing what ripples a repeated word, or, in the case of the villanelle, a repeated line, sends out, not on the surface but through the body of a text."[8] Her "Villanelle for D.G.B." in *Presentation Piece*, the Lamont Poetry Selection for 1973 and National Book Award winner in poetry for 1975, offers several examples of widely varied nuance in meaning for the refrain lines, despite very little change in wording.

> Every day our bodies separate,
> exploded torn and dazed.
> Not understanding what we celebrate

we grope through languages and hesitate
and touch each other, speechless and amazed;
and every day our bodies separate

us farther from our planned, deliberate
ironic lives. I am afraid, disphased,
not understanding what we celebrate

when our fused limbs and lips communicate
the unlettered power we have raised.
Every day our bodies' separate

routines are harder to perpetuate.
In wordless darkness we learn wordless praise,
not understanding what we celebrate;

wake to ourselves, exhausted, in the late
morning as the wind tears off the haze,
not understanding how we celebrate
our bodies. Every day we separate.[9]

In this examination of the ironies of communicating, both by touch and by language, Hacker indulges in semantic legerdemain of the sort for which the loose-lined villanelle seems peculiarly suited. Earlier writers in the form would allow an occasional elided syllable, but dropping four syllables from what is basically a decasyllabic line (as in the second line of this poem) amounts to a considerable departure from convention. The justification for the elision may be that exploding the metrics at this point is a functional means of emphasizing the explosion and dazzlement of the lovers' separation. The problem, however, is that the conventional line has not been fully established when the break occurs. Had the rupture been delayed for the second or some later stanza, its impact might have been greater.

Much of the semantic play in this poem has to do with the first (A¹) refrain line. First, the bodies separate from each other, leaving the lovers uncertain as to what their love is. The conceptual and dramatic circumstances are similar to those which one encounters in some of John Donne's aubades and valedictions. Next, the bodies separate the lovers ("us") from their rational lives. The sexual union is not fully understandable; its language is an "unlettered power." Then, in the fourth stanza, the verb "separate" is changed to its adjectival function. The "separate/routine" of the lovers' bodies becomes more difficult to sustain each day as the mystery of their love, in its "wordless darkness," continues to defy comprehension. Finally, the second refrain line undergoes an important alteration, from "what we celebrate" to "how we celebrate," and the verb acquires, for the first time, a direct object, "our bodies." Like Merrill (above), Hacker introduces a caesura in the closing couplet to provide a crucial shift in meaning. Whereas the poem begins with the separation of bodies, it concludes with the separation of selves.

In two other villanelles, "Ruptured Friendship, *or*, The High Cost of Keys" and "Villanelle: Late Summer" (in *Separations*, 1976), Marilyn Hacker returns to the comic use of the form. "Villanelle: Late Summer" also concerns a problem of communication between a man and a woman, but the circumstances are quite unlike those of "Villanelle for D.G.B." as the last stanza indicates:

> And I am grimly silent, swollen full
> of unsaid things. I certainly can't say
> "I love you." And it makes me rather dull.
> The conversation hits a certain lull.[10]

More broadly humorous, as the title suggests, is "Ruptured Friendships." The second stanza illustrates the playfulness of this villanelle:

> Tonight's ragout would be a mess
> without the red clay casserole
> I am obliged to repossess.[11]

Hacker's use of the shorter, octosyllabic line for this poem tends to emphasize the lighter mood.

Rachel Hadas, whose villanelles reflect the influence of James Merrill's loose-lined technique, observes that the form "contains an essence of lyric (not narrative) poetry, a meditative circling and returning to the same point or points."[12] "Pale Cast," published in *The Harvard Advocate* in 1976, stresses the relapsing nature of the villanelle in its continual outward–inward movement.

> Craving for clarity in what we see
> we'd color shapes. The prettiness of pain
> pursues us from the outside as inwardly.
>
> This muted landscape, unmistakably
> (though speckled through the windows of the train)
> craving for clarity, in what we see
>
> of rusted weed or bleached extent of tree
> fails of firm outline. Dullness like a stain
> pursues us from outside, as inwardly

hurt blurs perception of the symmetry
of passion, and unfolded ends remain
craving for clarity. In what we see

of Indiana's anonymity,
a wish to rape to radiance this grain
pursues us from outside as inwardly.

External dimness spreads obscurity
within; the dark heart darkens all again.
Craving for clarity in what we see
pursues us from outside as inwardly.[13]

More than most writers of the villanelle, but reminiscent in some ways
of Roethke, Hadas develops the aural potential of the form so that the
repetition involves sound as well as concept and refrain. Sometimes, as
with the alliterative phrases (e.g., "craving for clarity," "the prettiness of
pain/pursues"), the effects are obvious. Her use of assonance is sometimes more subtle: "of rusted weed or bleached extent of the tree"; "hurt
blurs perception"; " to rape to radiance this grain." Of the eighteen pro-
spective lines in this poem, twelve are enjambed, and in three cases,
across stanzas.

The desire for "clarity," implicitly for the persona in the poem,
amounts to the desire for certainty about love. By implication, again,
such certainty would provide her with clarity about other things. It is
the dullness "outside" that needs clarifying as much as the inward uncer-
tainty; the landscape appears to call out for definition. The "symmetry/of
passion" has been blurred, but perhaps if she could clarify the external
she could also clarify the internal. The forceful reference to rape suggests, figuratively at least, that a painful "radiance" is preferable to the
"External dimness" which "spreads obscurity/within." The wit of this
poem results from the assertion that people are not alone in their need
for "clarity": the phenomenal world outside us, to which we also belong,
at least in part, also craves "clarity." The occasional ambiguity in this
poem is an intentional expression of the paradox by which distinctions
between outer and inner are denied.

The loose- or free-lined villanelles of poets like Merrill, Hacker,
and Hadas are perhaps responsible for some of the experiments with
the form that have become fairly common over the past ten years. Or
from another perspective, one might date the experimentation from the
earliest modifications of Jean Passerat's model. As noted in Chapter 3,
above, Théodore de Banville, in reviving the form in 1845, expanded

the number of stanzas by two, and Maurice Rollinat was to multiply that expansion several times. Leconte de Lisle in one case dropped two tercets from Passerat's model, and in another he modified the rhyme pattern. Austin Dobson toyed with measure and Ernest Dowson was using slant-rhyme in his villanelles in the early 1890's. In some ways, however, it is Ezra Pound's "free-form" villanelle, an attempt to capture the spirit of the form, that lies behind the experimentation of contemporary poets, who have gone so far as to produce the "prose villanelle."

Gilbert Sorrentino's untitled villanelle in *The Perfect Fiction* (1968) exemplifies one type of experiment, the rejection of a standard rhythmic base.

> There is no instance that was not love:
> at one time
> or another. The seasons move
>
> into the past. The seasons shove
> one another away, sunshine or rime—
> there is no instance that was not love,
>
> one kind or another. Rough
> winds at us all now, one kind
> or another. The seasons move
>
> away from birds; jays, doves:
> or they fly into them, fly, climb,
> no instance that was not love.
>
> It is not just some scent on a glove
> nor a glittering coin, a dime
> or another: the seasons move
>
> unerringly, stolid and bluff.
> One would like to find
> one instance that was not love;
> another;
>   the seasons
>   move — [14]

Sorrentino takes considerable liberties with rhyme, and the broken refrain line in the last stanza, in which the line "moves" just as the seasons do, constitutes a notable departure from conventional form. Despite the frequent use of enjambment, the poem is somehow fitful. Obviously the variation of line length, from three syllables (discounting the last three lines) to ten, and the lack of a metric base do contribute to the roughness which the words announce, but so, too, does the heavy application of caesura. The seasonal movement is "rough": the seasons "shove/one another away." Love appears to be omnipresent, but always receding with time, always stated in the past tense.

Richard Hugo's villanelle in *What Thou Lovest Well, Remains American* (1975) is, he says, "impure": "It's like any form, I suppose, in that it forces the poet to transfer the mind's rigidity from substance to process, thus letting the substance go ignored for the moment, giving it a chance to grow—the way children will grow if their parents don't pay *too much* attention to them."[15]

> The dim boy claps because the others clap.
> The polite word, handicapped, is muttered in the stands.
> Isn't it wrong, the way the mind moves back.
>
> One whole day I sit, contrite, dirt, L.A.
> Union Station, '46, sweating through last night.
> The dim boy claps because the others clap.
>
> Score, 5 to 3. Pitcher fading badly in the heat.
> Isn't it wrong to be or not be spastic?
> Isn't it wrong, the way the mind moves back.
>
> I'm laughing at a neighbor girl beaten to scream
> by a savage father and I'm ashamed to look.
> The dim boy claps because the others clap.
>
> The score is always close, the rally always short.
> I've left more wreckage than a quake.
> Isn't it wrong, the way the mind moves back.
>
> The afflicted never cheer in unison.
> Isn't it wrong, the way the mind moves back
> to stammering pastures where the picnic should have worked.
> The dim boy claps because the others clap.[16]

One might classify this villanelle, "The Freaks at Spurgin Road Field," as a poem in the spirit of the villanelle. In some ways it is further from the conventional form than Sorrentino's poem, and in other ways it is closer. The most striking departure from convention is Hugo's rejection of schematic rhyme, the refrain lines having only the assonance of the last words in common. The line length varies from eight to thirteen syllables, and the refrain lines are redistributed in the last stanza. Nevertheless, there is much of the essence of the villanelle in this poem, including the tendency of the most conventional writers toward generally end-stopped lines. Against the disharmony of the "freaks," the heat, the "savage father," the refrain lines assert a sort of unity and order, in part because while most other lines in the poem vary in syllabic count, the refrain lines are uniformly decasyllabic and essentially iambic. The phrase, "mind moves back," shifts in meaning from the memory of the speaker to the mind of the retarded boy. The "dim boy claps" apparently (given the intentional ambiguity of the fourth tercet) at the screaming girl "because the others clap." Clearly the "freaks" at the ballpark include at least "the dim boy," the "savage father," and the speaker himself.

William Pitt Root's unpublished "Terrorist from the Heartland" does not appear on the page to be a villanelle at all, since he does not use the tercet structure, but the poem is nineteen lines long and two refrain lines alternate, though one appears only three times. I give the poem here as a further example of experimentation with the villanelle form.

> I am the memory you have not recalled
> since burying the stunning blood, tucking in
> the edges of the grass like a child
> tucks in the favored plastic doll, dead
> to its deathliness, its rigorous grin.
>
> I am the memory you have not recalled
> and do not wish to know now though I've called
> you by your secret name, my shrill voice thin
> as edges of the grass. Like a child
> I call you — softly, softly — small hands chilled
> by dread from that dream we, *only we*, have known.
>
> I am the memory you have not recalled
> nor dared recall, you who have tried to build
> all your years on this hollow place eaten
> by edges of the grass. Like a coiled
> relic, mineral-eyed, hypnotic, my countenance as old
> as Fear become rude weapon, dung turned to stone,
> I am the memory you have not recalled
> calling you now, as you go pale, grow cold.[17]

The use of the villanelle form for a poem pertaining to memory seems fitting, with its recurring refrain suggestive, especially in this case, of a memory continually forcing itself into consciousness. Root has a more conventional villanelle, "Malfunction," which appeared in his first book, *The Storm* (1969). In that villanelle Root writes in tercets, but the "a" rhymes are assonantal throughout: spasm/that/fat/lapses/fact/attack/sack.[18]

New York poet Karen Swenson's "I Have Lost the Address of My Country" also involves about as much rejection of convention as it does adoption. Perhaps it is best to consider this poem, set up in quatrains and five lines longer than the usual villanelle, as one influenced by the form.

> "I have lost the address of my country,"
> my friend says, her voice soft in her mouth
> as barefoot dust on the streets of Persepolis and Bam—
> dust baked to the hard bricks of old mosques.
>
> In a bar in Indiana I watch
> the square guarded by lupin spires of minarets
> boil with a mass like krill before the jaws of a whale.
> "I have lost the address of my country."
>
> The night after the women strike
> burn their chadors, their black winding clothes
> we talk half the night our voices hard
> as dust baked to the bricks of old mosques.
>
> I've had no address for a year but car and suitcase
> knowing only road, a typewriter ribbon
> spilled out over mountain and plain,
> trying to find the address of my self's country.
>
> And I've felt my life blown, tumbleweed
> before headlights in Wyoming or dust off the Colorado flats
> and I have feared that I will be
> dust baked to the hard bricks of old mosques.
>
> I come home to hear her voice gentle
> as the eroded profiles of Persepolis whose 6,000 years of
> dust is baked to the hard bricks of old mosques,
> "I have lost the address of my country."[19]

Swenson uses the alternating refrain lines of the villanelle form to mark the transitions between the "I" of the poem and the Iranian friend, both of whom have lost their country, but in different ways. Compared with Root's poem, Swenson's shows a more conventional application of refrain lines and, despite the quatrains, a stanzaic development which is closer to that of the conventional villanelle.

Both Root and Swenson consider their poems to be villanelles, and the alternating refrain lines appear to be the key feature of the form to them. Although Denise Levertov does not, so far as I know, consider "Obsessions" to be a villanelle, there are intriguing similarities.

Maybe it is true we have to return
to the black air of ashcan city
because it is there the most life was burned,

as ghosts or criminals return?
But no, the city has no monopoly
of intense life. The dust burned

golden or violet in the wide land
to which we ran away, images
of passion sprang out of the land

as whirlwinds or red flowers, your hands
opened in anguish or clenched in violence
under that sun, and clasped my hands

in that place to which we will not return
where so much happened that no one else noticed,
where the city's ashes that we brought with us
flew into the intense sky still burning.[20]

The poem is set up in tercets (one less than the usual villanelle) with a concluding quatrain, so that it has the appearance of a villanelle on the page. Moreover, perhaps because the poem has to do with an obsessive desire to return, there is some emphasis on repetition. The key words, "return" and "burn(ing)," reecho throughout the poem, though not as typical villanelle refrains. I mention the poem here primarily by way of indicating that the villanelle might well be of some influence on form aside from the refrain lines.

Of the experiments conducted with the villanelle during the past few years, one of the most unusual is the prose villanelle. Barbara Lefcowitz, whose work in the form was influenced by that of Philip Stevick, defines the prose villanelle as "nineteen sentences written with the same pattern of repetition one finds in the conventional villanelle, but without rhyme."[21] Unfortunately Lefcowitz's prose villanelle, published in *Gallimaufry* (1977), and Stevick's, in *The Chicago Review* (1976) with three other "mannered pieces" (two rondeaus and a triolet in prose), are too long to reproduce here. Some sense of how the form operates, however, can be gleaned from Judith Johnson Sherwin's "Another Story," identified as a prose villanelle, in *How the Dead Count* (1978).

i saw a tree. i couldn't find you. you were going to eat me.

the refrigerator looked empty. i didn't know what to do. i
looked out at the tree.

you looked hungry. i thought we were through but now you wanted
to eat me.

it wasn't easy to do. i looked at the tree.

we moved up so slowly. halfway through, you got me.

if i could have pulled free i could have saved you. i was almost
up the tree when you ate me.[22]

Lefcowitz and Sherwin have also written verse villanelles, both taking
considerable liberties with the form.[23]

With the prose villanelle, experimentation has been pushed to its
limit. Certainly future villanelles will reflect the impact of the loose-
lined and the experimental versions. After attracting some thematic
flexibility in the works of such poets as John Davidson and E. A.
Robinson, it was perhaps just a matter of time before poets began to
test out the flexibility of the form itself. The first important break-
through was the use of slant- and eye-rhyme, general acceptance of
which begins after Theodore Roethke's "The Waking." Then, with James
Merrill and poets of lesser renown leading the way, the villanelle acquired
flexibility of line. From there it has been a short step to more radical,
and some might even say "destructive," manipulations. The conventional villanelle, however, is not likely to die. Within just a few months
of my writing this sentence, Christopher Millis's "Ceremony" was published in *Cutbank*, a reminder not only of the vitality of the conventional
form, but also of its thematic range.[24]

◆

Appendix A
The Villanelle and the Poet

*T*here will always be those who agree with Marjorie Boulton, in *The Anatomy of Poetry*, that the villanelle is "A highly artificial form, so repetitive that it generally says very little," that because of its technical complexity it takes up "an amount of space in a reference book quite out of all proportion" to its importance.[1] Part of the intent of this study has been to challenge that view. I knew from the outset about many of the really fine efforts in the form by such poets as Auden, Thomas, and Roethke. I soon discovered a number of rather trivial villanelles, in which the form was achieved and little else. I hypothesized that the form was too easy in one sense and too difficult in another, to produce a middle ground of "solid" poems. Initial research turned up many more accomplished villanelles by sophisticated poets and many more examples of triviality. Villanelles kept showing up in books like *Poetry is Fun*, *The Fireside Book of Humorous Poetry*, *The Hollow Reed*, and *A Whimsey Anthology*. Some were awful.

In order to discover whether there was a "middle ground" and to acquire some information of the sort that only poets can supply, I ran an announcement of my project in *Coda*, a nationally distributed newsletter for poets and writers published with the support of the National Endowment for the Arts.[2] The response to my call for information about villanelles and for comments on the strengths and weaknesses of the form and problems encountered in writing it was gratifying. I had anticipated that ten to twenty poets might respond, but over forty, from Alaska to Florida, sent work and comments. For the anthology of villanelles which follows, I was able to select from well over a hundred poems, most of which had already been published in literary journals or magazines. I am satisfied that a substantial body of villanelles written in English now exists, and I am impressed that the quality of the work is sufficient to deny my hypothesis.

Several of the comments offered by poets who have been writing villanelles recently are of some interest. There was almost unanimous agreement among the respondents that the form was a "challenge." As Professor Imogene Bolls of Wittenberg University in Springfield, Ohio writes, "I still return to the villanelle when I feel that I need to send myself back to a school of keen discipline, to fight a clean fight, to prove again to myself that I have earned the right to *break* the rules."[3] Most of the poets who responded write primarily free verse, but they apparently regard fixed forms, and particularly the villanelle, as a way of "keeping honest" with the craft. Professor Carol Poster of Indiana University blames the literary and academic "establishment" for having set up a "tyranny of free verse," against which the villanelle might be a sort of protest,[4] and Jon Daunt (Gates Mills, Ohio) recommends the form to those "who do not fear self-discipline."[5]

While a degree of antagonism toward free verse on the part of the respondents was not unusual, most would probably agree with Poster that an interest in fixed forms often derives from "a sense of their freedom and flexibility" and that "before variation can become meaningful, a regular pattern must be established." Grace Morton of Cambridge, Massachusetts writes, the "sprung villanelle," which "uses repetition, but changes it as it progresses, gives a different type of drama—one that uses more of the element of surprise, less of inevitability."[6] Helen Saslow (Brooklyn, New York), who studied the villanelle with Gilbert Sorrentino, prefers the "scope that dissonance allows" to "absolute rhyming."[7] Barbara Lefcowitz (Bethesda, Maryland), who has done work in the prose villanelle, "almost always" takes "liberties with the villanelle refrain, sometimes repeating only a key word or sound."[8]

The challenge of the form, according to Alberto Ríos (Tucson, Arizona), is in the tendency of most poets to over-generalize in the refrain lines. "Of course, it is hard to repeat over and over a specific," Ríos states, but "I used several devices, enjambment being foremost, to make the repetition less obvious, or at least return repetition to its original intention: to change the refrain with each usage."[9] Joanne Seltzer (Schenectady, New York), who considers Ernest Dowson the master of the form and was among the very few respondents to recognize the work of the turn-of-the-century English poets, finds several "drawbacks" to the villanelle: the tendency to end-stop lines, the flatness of the final couplet, and the difficulty of correcting imperfections in the first draft.[10] Carol Poster and many others who comment on the form agree that the redundancy of the refrain is itself the form's greatest weakness. "There are very few perceptions which seem to demand the form," writes Poster, and the refrains are often not strong enough to bear the stress of reiteration. She suggests two ways of avoiding this: "The first is composing two stunningly brilliant incantatory lines and steadily building in intensity around them. . . . The second involves composing two fairly unobtrusive lines which gain power as the poem progresses." The worst villanelles, notes Poster, are those in which the refrain lines become obtrusive as a result of attempted profundity: "In verse as in society, you can get away with anything as long as you're reasonably discreet about it."

As Poster's comments suggest, the villanelle can provide a useful text for the study of poetic form and of the relationship in literature between form and content. Mary J. J. Wrinn's observations on the villanelle in *The Hollow Reed* (1935) involve advice on use of the form in the classroom, and her anthology includes some villanelles by high school students.[11] Several respondents indicated that they had used the villanelle in teaching creative writing and introductory poetry classes. Harold Bond (Melrose, Massachusetts) reports that he has been teaching the villanelle for years in his poetry writing classes at the Cambridge Center for Adult Education,[12] and Billie Jean James of the University of Nevada indicates success with "modified villanelles" in the Poets-In-The-Schools (PITS) programs.[13] James Dickey, resident poet at the University of South Carolina, spends much of the first semester of his poetry-writing courses on fixed forms, including the villanelle.[14] The most interesting classroom use of the form may be that of Sanford Pinsker of Franklin and Marshall College in Lancaster, Pennsylvania. In teaching James Joyce's *A Portrait of the Artist as a Young Man*, he decided to involve his class in the "aesthetic turmoil" of Stephen Dedalus in his composition of the "Villanelle of the Temptress" in the fifth chapter. "Before anybody could knock poor Stephen and his Swinburnian poem," they were required to turn out their own villanelle. For some, Pinsker says, it was a sobering experience. "Somehow," he concludes, "Stephen's effort did not seem as creaky as it once had."[15]

Pinsker's experiment "also suggested that the form of the villanelle is, indeed, congenial to certain modes of meditation, that the form is integral with function." Other poets also detected significant relationships between form and content in their work with the villanelle. In some cases, the villanelle form was seen as a way of handling stubborn content. Marilyn Folkestad (Portland, Oregon) writes: "I had all kinds of information for this poem, but had never been able to hook it to a framework that made it work, so I decided to try to use a strict form — I could concentrate on the form and the ideas could take care of themselves."[16] As Philip Dacey of Southwest State University in Marshall, Minnesota observes, "The great challenge of the villanelle (like the challenge of all intricate French forms) is to keep the obvious artifice of the poem from swamping the poem's credibility; in other words, a believable human voice must be there, despite the highly artificial structure."[17] "But therein lies the pleasure," according to Helen Saslow, "to make the form bend without loss, to make the content more independent of the form." Finally, as Harald Wyndham (Pocatello, Idaho) puts it, "Villanelles give you one hell of a challenge — how to make them come out natural and smooth, without the glaring machinery sticking out and drawing attention to itself."[18]

As Pinsker's experiment showed, however, many poets find the villanelle form particularly useful for certain kinds of thematic statements and tones. Pinsker was not alone in finding the form appropriate for meditative subjects, and Folkestad found it well suited to a certain quality of fantasy in her poem. The most commonly mentioned conceptual link was, predictably, with repeated action and time. Annette Hayn (Queens Village, New York) notes: "It seemed the best way to express the passage of time, the repetitions of the wish from the past versus the irrevocable changes caused by aging."[19] Theodore Hall (New Concord, Ohio) writes: "I like the form because it's consonant with my sense of history — as incrementally repetitive, yet, finally, unpredictable."[20] Dorothy Foltz-Gray (Morristown, Tennessee) finds that "the form adds an evocative feeling and the subject of nature's cycle is enhanced by the villanelle's cyclical form."[21] Similar to these views is that of Joanna Cattonar, who has taught in New Mexico and South Carolina: "I searched for different forms and chose the villanelle because it promised an apt frame and *momentum*."[22]

A number of respondents found the villanelle particularly well suited to the expression of conflict or tension of various sorts. Duane Carr (El Paso, Texas) suggests that while the sonnet often satisfies his need to work toward resolution, "I do feel there are some conflicts that very often are not resolved, and for this the villanelle serves."[23] "What I hope for," writes California poet George Keithley, "is the suggestion of opposites which require each other—structure and freedom, convention and innovation—in a poem about winter and spring, death and love."[24] Imogene Bolls uses the villanelle "to create tension between serious content and a tight, sometimes (historically) light form."

Obviously, different poets have discovered many other conceptual connections between the villanelle form and various themes. Theodore Hall, for example, was guided in choosing the form for an enigmatic dream poem by Donald Justice's "preference for the more elaborate traditional forms when working with the most irrational materials." Several poets wrote at some length on the composition of a particular villanelle. Grace Morton's "Leopards and the Artist," originally published in *The Mississippi Review*, is one example.

> We hear the leopards pacing in the hall;
> their breath dampens the priceless draperies,
> softly, softly their black paws lift and fall.
>
> The rosewood thickness of our bedroom wall
> can't shield us. Through parquets, beams, galleries,
> we hear the leopards pacing in the hall;
>
> and all we know, the leopard learns, and all
> our gilt barriers give. They go where they please,
> softly, softly, their slim paws lift and fall.
>
> Their bony rhythm is not beautiful,
> we dread to hear their muscles cock and ease,
> we fear the leopards crouching in the hall.
>
> Don't listen! Outside, poppies line the mall;
> by garden gates there hang no tapestries
> where restlessly the bright claws scrape and fall;
>
> But tapestries may show jungles, and tall,
> humid black cats that quicken, that release
> the trapped and splendid leopards in the hall.
> Listen! Listen! The treadles rise and fall.[25]

Of this poem, which she calls a "sprung villanelle," Morton writes: "Here the villanelle form was to emphasize the pacing, locked up movement of the leopards; 'spring' was given to the ending to emphasize the freedom and change when leopards are seen in this new way. Within the strict rhyme I occasionally used a slight variation, namely 'beautiful' and 'release'; the first was to emphasize the awkwardness of the bony rhythm; the second was to emphasize the sudden freedom."

The foregoing has been a summary of the views of some twenty poets and teachers of poetry as to the nature of the villanelle, its strengths and weaknesses. It represents less than half of the total responses I received, but the comments amount to a fair sample of the consensus. Respondents were also asked to indicate whose work in the form had influenced their own, and although the names Dylan Thomas and Theodore Roethke were listed most often, many others were mentioned: Ernest Dowson, Oscar Wilde, E. A. Robinson, James Joyce, W. H. Auden, Ezra Pound, Weldon Kees, Sylvia Plath, Gilbert Sorrentino, Philip Stevick, Marilyn Hacker. Although several respondents indicated their awareness of the French origins of the form, not one mentioned the name of Jean Passerat, the poet who gave it definition at the end of the sixteenth century, or the French poets who revived it in the nineteenth century. In general, however, the poets showed themselves alert to the potential and to the problems of the form.

Appendix B
Poems Reprinted in the Text

Sixty-seven villanelles are included in complete form in the text of this book. They constitute a sort of historical anthology of the subject. The list below includes all of those poems with the exception of the two- or three-lined Spanish *estribillos*. Italian, French, and Spanish versions are also included. Where a title other than "Villanelle" is available, I have used that and placed it in quotation marks; otherwise, I have written out the first line of the poem. Most of the Italian villanelles (villanelle) are anonymous.

Appendix C
A Contemporary Anthology

*T*he following 33 villanelles, including one prose villanelle, exemplify the work presently being done in the form, most of these poems having been published within the past ten years. Some are published here for the first time. While I have made no effort to favor "name" poets in making my selections, most of which are from poems submitted in response to my announcement in *Coda* magazine in 1978, a number of the poets do have established reputations. Three of the poems are among the thirteen villanelles reprinted in Philip Dacey and David Jauss's *Strong Measures: Contemporary American Poetry in Traditional Forms* (New York: Harper & Row, 1986), which also includes villanelles by such well known poets as Stephen Dunn, Peter Klappert, and Donald Justice. The slight overlapping is coincidental.

I have attempted no close organization of the poems in this miniature anthology, but in general I have started with those concerning love, then death, following with poems pertaining to various individuals or "characters," and concluding with those involving an event or a place. Adherence to the traditional form varies from the strict formalism of Norman N. McWhinney's "Truth Lies in Paradox" to the nonstanzaic villanelle, "La Sequiá/The Drought," by Alberto Ríos. The selections are my own, based upon what I hope by now is a well-informed perspective on what is being done these days with the villanelle.

Poets represented: Elizabeth Bishop, Imogene L. Bolls, Harold Bond, Joanna Cattonar, Ann Fox Chandonnet, Philip Dacey, Madeline DeFrees, Marilyn Folkestad, Charles Guenther, Theodore Hall, Edward Harkness, Annette Hayn, Bonnie Cochrane Hirsch, Rolfe Humphries, Phyllis Janowitz, George Keithley, Christopher Millis, Carolyn Kizer,

Barbara Lefcowitz, Norman N. McWhinney, Howard Nemerov, William Packard, Henry Petroski, Alberto Ríos, Helen Saslow, Kim Robert Stafford, David Wagoner, John Wain, Jeanne Murray Walker, Celeste Turner Wright, Charles David Wright, and Harald Wyndham.

If April

If April is to green the earth again
Rock Lake will shudder and unlock its sighs
when love lies down with death in the dark rain

easing the ice, so the slow floes drain
into the swollen stream. We'll hear it rise
if April is to green the earth again

where the willows stir, shaking that satin sheen
from their stiff skirts, the fine snow from our eyes.
Though love lies deep with death in the dark rain

rumpling their bed, on the blue mud we've seen
the first loon wade, or waddle, before he flies.
If April is to green the earth again

soon will that demon deep-diving loon
shatter the water with his witless cries.
Must love lie still as doom in this dark rain?

The lake's awake! We hear the hooting loon
loud, loud, beneath our somber skies —
If April is to green the earth again,
Love, we'll lie warm and laugh in the dark rain.

George Keithley

Truth Lies in Paradox

Truth lies in paradox, but touch is real.
The oaks applaud, the wind says "Yes" to love.
The golden light is never heard to feel.

The time to wound is still the time to heal.
The memory's a scar that's made of love.
Truth lies in paradox, but touch is real.

All our hands are touching in their appeal,
The lightly touching fingertips of love
The golden light is never heard to feel.

Shout "love" and "Love" and "LOVE" with all your zeal!
No echo ever will say more than *love.*

Truth lies in paradox, but touch is real.

The silence of this line will well reveal
The absence of all listening to our love.
The golden light is never heard to feel.

Since all our words are mortal, I'll conceal
In ink a formula for ever-love.
Truth lies in paradox, but touch is real;
The golden light was never heard to feel.

Norman N. McWhinney

A Walk in the Country (near Altea, Spain)

We left the road for where the clover grew
To wade surprised in clover to our knees:
The clover bed was deeper than we knew.

Since we'd been walking for an hour or two
And since the clover bowed so in the breeze,
We left the road for where the clover grew.

We ate our lunch of red wine, bread, a few
Apples, and some green olives stuffed with cheese
In clover reaching deeper than we knew.

Austin laughing pulled clover that he threw
At Emmet as he dreamed under orange trees
Plumping their burden where the clover grew.

Then I joined in and threw clover at you,
Who laughed to show how soft assaults can please
(And show the bed was deeper than we knew).

Soon we were all fighting—the green spears flew!—
But we were only clover-enemies
Who left a road for where the clover grew
To play in clover deeper than we knew.

Philip Dacey

Villanelle to Wake my Love

You lie in bed behind the silent door
while birds already gossip with the leaves.
The day awakes; my Love, we knew before.

Outside the window, morning wishes fire
casually on the moss that clings to trees.
You lie in bed behind the silent door.

And green the fields fling and snap in air;
green rings the smell, alfalfa, on the breeze.
Awake, my Love, the day we knew before.

And running griefless are the blessed deer
in freckled shade, on piccolo quick knees.
You lie in bed behind the silent door.

The day's my Love. The night's a dreamless boor
who pays off social debts and earns degrees.
Awake, my Love, the day we knew before.

The sun in you perhaps will rise once more,
rise and perhaps default the dark with ease.
You lie in bed behind the silent door.
My Love, awake the day we knew before.

                                    Jeanne Murray Walker

If Our Minds Mated as Our Bodies Do

If our minds mated as our bodies do,
doubtless I'd be content to learn and tell—
inserting keys in locks and walking through.

Thought is a mirror the thinker slips through
like Alice, pilgrim waltzing into Hell—
if our minds mated as our bodies do.

Sex is a mirror that lovers slide through
like water, and do not learn, but swell;
you insert key in lock—and enter you.

I'd be the scabbard and you the knife, blue
steel, well tempered—you the tongue, I the bell—
if our minds mated as our bodies do.

The mind's ungentle as it strives to do
the body in, rip nucleus from cell,
inserting keys in locks and walking through.

Like love, poems strive to caress, renew,
to give (before its death) body a bell—
when our minds mate as our bodies do,
inserting keys in locks and walking through.

                                    Ann Fox Chandonnet

Villanelle: Night Watch

Alone at night we face
the faces we survive;
a world we can't get past:

moving shadows, they exist
on cold corners, grieve
alone at night. Each face

wordless, speaks of the waste.
Their eyes, dead or alive
give us a world all ice.

Things slip, piece by piece;
fingers from a glove
at night. Alone we face

those nervous shadows, our lost
selves; and dreaming, crave
a world once filled with promise

now walled with sad ghosts
who follow in the wake of love.
Alone at night we face
its loss: the world: our past.

Helen Saslow

On a Line from Sophocles

I see you cruel, you find me less than fair.
Too kind to keep apart, we two brutes meet.
Time, time, my friend, makes havoc everywhere.

Our stammers left to hunger in the air
Like smoke or music, turn the weather sweet:
To seek us, cruel; to find us, less than fair.

Testing our own reflections unaware
Each caught an image that was once conceit.
Time, time, my friend, makes havoc everywhere.

Eyes lewd for spotting death in life declare
That fallen flesh reveals the skull: complete.
I see you. Cruel. You find me less than fair.

The sacking of the skin, the ashen hair—
But more than surfaces compound the cheat!
Time, time, my friend, makes havoc *everywhere*

The years betray our vows to keep and care.
O traitors! ugly in this last defeat,
I find you cruel, you see me less than fair.
Time, time, my friend, makes havoc everywhere.

Carolyn Kizer

Wearing Well

What precious little does against despair.
Sun takes the ground and flourishes on stone,
I brace my heart upon the morning air.

The coffee tells, the sycamore is there,
and real things hold their places on their own.
What precious little does against despair.

The keen of questions and their edge's wear
have rasped away the night over a hone.
I brace my heart upon the morning air,

breathing it in, while it cajoles my hair
admonishing me, for I should have known
what precious little does against despair.

Night's slow erosion and the day's repair
should be familiar now. Starting alone,
I brace my heart upon the morning air.

Sufficient unto the day, to hold and bear,
life steadies in essential root and bone.
What precious little does against despair.
I brace my heart upon the morning air.

Charles David Wright

Planting Cacti in Jars Saved from the Farm Dump

She has lost her private wars
which these old magazines once helped her wage.
Among the empty cold cream jars,

half-buried near the wild sunflowers,
there's a rusty cage.
She has lost her private wars.

A solitary perfume bottle cowers
under half-dead sage
among the empty cold cream jars.

Vitamin bottles gave up powers

she could not gauge.
She has lost her private wars.

Every four hours
prescriptions crack again from age
among the empty cold cream jars.

Anything that stays here sours.
Mud rots away the final page.
She has lost her private wars
among the empty cold cream jars.

Bonnie Hirsch

Blue Villanelle

In dream I dug a hole for you
So calm you stepped into it
And the sky turned perfectly blue

You motioned me to bury you
I tried to talk you out of it
In dream I dug a hole for you

I shoveled my fear upon you
With dark relief you received it
And the sky turned perfectly blue

I remember your eyes went blue
The white oval of your face lit
In dream I dug a hole for you

When finished I knelt upon you
I touched the fresh earth with my lips
And the sky turned perfectly blue

For months I have stood over you
Not knowing what will come of it
In dream I dug a hole for you
And the sky turned perfectly blue

Theodore Hall

The Way You Are

I wanted to grow up the way you are
But now you're old. I'm leaving you behind
In a pink nursing home tied to a chair.

What's left of you can only shake and stare.
You bit the nurse and push away my hand.

I wanted to grow up the way you are.

I loved your gentleness and lack of fear
But what I loved I cannot find
In a pink nursing home tied to a chair.

Helpless I mourned your many deaths before
The final one. You used to understand
I wanted to grow up the way you are.

No one converses any more.
Each patient fights his private fiend
In a pink nursing home tied to a chair.

The silence in this day-room is bizarre.
You are alone, abandoned at the end
In a pink nursing home tied to a chair.
I wanted to grow up the way you are.

Annette Hayn

Villanelle: The Dying Man

I am prepared to leave this house today.
I keep my travel-bag beneath my bed.
Each night I dream about the broad highway.

I have outgrown these rooms. Why should I stay?
My kids are gone. My wife and friends are dead.
I've half a mind to leave this house today.

Inside things fall to pieces and decay.
My nerves are held together by a thread.
Each night I dream about the broad highway.

Although I swore I'd make that old man pay
the price of seventy years upon my head,
for fifty cents I'd leave this house today.

Just like a boy who wants to run away,
impatient for the wind-blown open road,
I dream each night about the broad highway.

But I do nothing. What is there to say?
The moment faces me with secret dread.
I am afraid to leave this house today.
Each night I dream about the broad highway.

Harald Wyndham

Dying is a Matter of Degrees

Dying is a matter of degrees.
We watch the worst come to others,
Never seeing what the others see,

While summers thaw and winters freeze:
A lifelong erosion. Like weather,
Dying is a matter of degrees.

The dying wander never where they please,
Trailing bedclothes into halls, and never,
Never seeing what the others see:

Fingers fumbling at the throat, pleas
Crumbling to coughing, fever
(Dying is a matter of degrees).

Flesh fallen sinks to knees
Gnarled and shriveled, shrinks to cover,
Never seeing what the others see.

What the falling body frees
Is invisible, and we see no further
Than that dying is a matter of degrees,
Never knowing what the other sees.

                                   Imogene L. Bolls

The Teacher of Poetry

O what a lovely poem, Mrs. Jones.
One really has to read it once or twice.
And there are no disturbing overtones.

You say God's garden has all sorts of stones.
How pious, how incisive, how concise!
O what a lovely poem, Mrs. Jones.

You say God's flowers are our chaperones.
How civilized, and what a nice device!
And there are no disturbing overtones.

You say God's grace is like eau de cologne.
How apt, and how delightfully precise!
O what a lovely poem, Mrs. Jones.

You say we should be holy in our bones.
How gay, to have this taste of paradise!
And there are no disturbing overtones.

You do not deal with any vague unknowns.
You make your point, and give quite wise advice.
O what a lovely poem, Mrs. Jones.
And there are no disturbing overtones.

William Packard

Villanelle:
For Harpo Marx

True oracles say more than they suppose.
Your very dumbness makes your message clear.
The clown may speak what silent Hamlet knows.

A harmless droll is what the camera shows,
The children's friend whom parents need not fear.
True oracles say more than they suppose.

In your fake world of frantic gag and pose
We see our real despair come striding near.
The clown may speak what silent Hamlet knows.

Your wasteful slapstick is a dig at those
Whose cash can buy the strength that most revere.
True oracles say more than they suppose.

You say that terror pays what pleasure owes.
What makes it real is that they cannot hear.
The clown may speak what silent Hamlet knows.

You tell them no man loves the dice he throws.
It is a zany world that calls you queer.
True oracles say more than they suppose.
The clown may speak what silent Hamlet knows.

John Wain

Self-Portrait

I am a metric man. I am. I am
A birthday anniversary of tears
Remembered by a yellow telegram

From relations. I feel a rocking pram,
Skip sidewalk cracks, and strike at rubber spheres:
I am a metric man, I am. I am

A chopped and channeled Deuce racing a cam
From zero to sixty in thrity years
Remembered by a yellow telegram

At graduation, Fifty words STOP. Cram
An eight-times-seven table down my ears:
I am a metric man, I am. I am

A birth controlled by every measured dram
Of moonlight, engagements of wristwatch gears
Remembered by a yellow telegram.

And now I count the days, the months, the . . . damn
Payments due, coffin nails, yards-to-go, the beers.
I am a metric man, I am. I am
Remembered by a yellow telegram.

Henry Petroski

Krumple the Landlord

It is only the tenants who would mind:
Krumple the landlord harps upon that theme.
He may himself believe it in the end.

Oko from Africa, suitcase in hand,
is canvassing the suburbs for a home.
It is only the tenants who would mind.

Krumple swears by the word which is his blond
he in his heart harbors all men the same.
He may himself believe it in the end.

Oko feels badly to see Krumple stand
embarrassed by his word. Struck deaf or dumb
it is only the tenants who would mind.

Krumple says that were Oko blue or blond
he would not be more grateful that he came.
He may himself believe it in the end,

if nothing else, when out of that dark land
riot and discontent is rumored from
the tongues only of tenants who would mind.
And they may all believe it in the end.

Harold Bond

Maggie

Tell about the circus again, will you?
I like the sound of sword and sawdust,
the tension of tiger, high wire and rope.

In the clean silence wrung from early storms,

we search the remarkable sign for a man
to tell us about the cirucs. Will you

point your rigid hands at dancing dogs?
The lady with the snakes amazed us that year.
When tension of tiger, high wire and rope

sagged down, her skin came off in strips.
A doll with changing heads costs ten nickels.
Tell about the cirucs again, will you?

And buy us cotton candy. Laugh and cringe.
Things settle in gutters. You care about
the tension of tiger, high wire and rope.

At the sultry end of summer, night men
struck the big top and you never married.
Tell about the circus again, will you,
the tension of tiger, high wire and rope?

Marilyn Folkestad

The Man in the Recreation Room

The man in the recreation room is screaming
again. From season to graveside the moon turns blue.
How unhappy. How his mind moves dreaming

something blue with passion: Three wings combing
space beyond a valley. What a view!
The man in the recreation room is screaming.

His hands have a mind of their own. He's palming
a gravestone. The moon has nothing to do.
How unhappy. How his mind moves dreaming

beyond a blue valley. His wings are flaming.
He's afraid his plans have fallen through,
the man in the recreation room screaming.

Past apples another starlight tries claiming
his eyesight. Flowers die. All untrue.
How unhappy now? His mind moves dreaming

His hands slowly become his feet. The humming
in his head grows beautiful. Just for you
the man in the recreation room is screaming.
How unhappy. How his mind moves dreaming.

Edward Harkness

Reprieve

You're somehow different: you believe,
No matter how misfortune mounts,
There always will be some reprieve.

The tangle-footed web you weave
Is just a trampoline to bounce:
You're somehow different, you believe.

You scribble checks on Christmas Eve
Against your overdrawn accounts;
There always will be some reprieve.

Clearly, your critics are naive,
Full of the faults that they denounce.
You're somehow different, you believe.

Age is a nuisance you deceive;
Wrinkles are foes that you can trounce;
There always will be some reprieve.

Though you may shake your head and grieve
When epidemics start to pounce,
You're somehow different, you believe:
There always will be some reprieve.

Celeste Turner Wright

Wilbur

The watch on his wrist and pulse are ticking together,
softly. Only Wilbur can hear them whisper,
"Go home Willie. No one wants you here."

Willie's wispy as filigree, resilient as wire.
And he's always on time. As if they were made for each other
the watch on his wrist and his pulse are sticking together.

Wilbur would like to assume a more casual air,
but his flimsy grin wears thin when he hears people swear,
"Go home Willie. No one wants you here."

He arranges to meet you under the clock at Zayre's.
And you're late. Or don't come. Maybe you don't even care.
The watch on his wrist and his pulse keep talking together.

Willie's no Weeper. He hopes that sooner or later
someone will touch him, someone too tender to sneer,
"Go home Willie. No one wants you here."

He can flit like a finch, a bunch of small bones and feathers,
but he knows how to wait. He'll wait for an hour or forever,
the watch on his wrist and his pulse beating together.

If blood leaks from his veins while he waits somewhere,
Willie will just go on waiting. He won't really care
that the watch on his wrist and his heart are unwinding together.
"Go home Willie no one wants you here."

Phyllis Janowitz

Ceremony

My father fishes when he's out of work
so early that he cannot see
his lines cast out into the dark.

He lights a cigarette, a spark
sets scales off in the sea.
My father fishes when he's out of work

and tries to wake me with a jerk
to the shoulder. "Get up. Get up," he coaxes softly.
His lines cast out into the dark

where I'm dreaming, like a shark
cuts water. He waits until I'm ready.
My father . . . Fishes when he's out of work!

As if by ceremony he could shirk
his sleepless nights, or convince me
his lines cast out into the dark

amount to something more than a mark
on water, more than a plea.
My father fishes when he's out of work.
His lines cast out into the dark.

Christopher Millis

Keeping Up with the Signs

Meadowlarks nesting March to August yield
to summer traffic in the dovetailed grass.
Three clear notes. Do Not Walk in Open Field.

I run the way my feet suggest. Upheld
by ringing turf and larkspur flash, I chase
meadowlarks nesting. March to August yield

sways heavy on the cornstalked land I flailed

to find the spot where larks come less and less.
Three clear notes do not walk. In open field,

runways the wind lays flat, fill up. Revealed
in the natural clutch called happiness:
meadowlarks' nesting march to August yield

in the tilt of wind, rainswell and the cold
mating ground, to bed with the dangerous
three. Clear notes do not walk in open field.

I leave five clues for the field guide whose wild
speculation turns the head. Shells express
meadowlarks' nesting march to august yield.
Three clear notes do not. Walk in open field.

Madeline DeFrees

La Sequía/The Drought

Peaches are drying up all around
Elfrida, Arizona. I must be
like my grandfather, without a sound
to show he's worried at all. His brown
hand rubs his elbow that feels like the
peaches are drying up all around
the pores and ridges of his skin and down
his back. My father used to do that. He,
like my grandfather, without a sound
of complaint, wore a fire that was blonde
on his head. He would say, too, "I can see
peaches are drying up all around,"
through the blue-eyed bruises he gave me,
like my grandfather, without a sound,
gave him one summer, one night on the ground
ripping apart the only thing he could. The
peaches are drying up all around
like my grandfather, without a sound.

Alberto Ríos

One Art

The art of losing isn't hard to master;
so many things seem filled with the intent
to be lost that their loss is no disaster.

Lose something every day. Accept the fluster
of lost door keys, the hour badly spent.
The art of losing isn't hard to master.

Then practice losing farther, losing faster:
places, and names, and where it was you meant
to travel. None of these will bring disaster.

I lost my mother's watch. And look! my last, or
next-to-last, of three loved houses went.
The art of losing isn't hard to master.

I lost two cities, lovely ones. And, vaster,
some realms I owned, two rivers, a continent.
I miss them, but it wasn't a disaster.

—Even losing you (the joking voice, a gesture
I love) I shan't have lied. It's evident
the art of losing's not too hard to master
though it may look like (*Write* it!) like disaster.

Elizabeth Bishop

Equations of a Villanelle

The breath within us is the wind without,
In interchange unnoticed all our lives.
What if the same be true of world and thought?

Air is the ghost that comes and goes uncaught
Through the great system of lung and leaf that sieves
The breath within us and the wind without;

And utterance, or inspiration going out,
Is borne on air, on empty air it lives
To say the same is true of world and thought.

This is the spirit's seamless fabric wrought
Invisible, whose working magic gives
The breath within us to the wind without.

O great wind, blow through us despite our doubt,
Distilling all life's sweetness in the hives
Where we deny the same to world and thought,

Till death, the candle guttering to naught,
Sequesters every self as it forgives
The breath within us for the wind without;
What if the same be true of world and thought?

Howard Nemerov

Sand Creek

Dark cuts the sun down as the season wills.
In this wild country
nothing lives long but the earth and the hills.

The wren's tongue stops its throat, the swaying gills
of fish shut, sudden wings slit the sky.
Dark cuts the sun down as the season wills.

Our children die and the branch fills.
Even our old songs cannot tell why
nothing lives long. But the earth and the hills

outlast our lives — though the rain stills
the silence, trees leaf fruit and die,
dark cuts the sun down. As the season wills,

young deer crowd before us and the sap spills,
days weigh like earth in our fingers, like dust lie:
nothing lives long but the earth and the hills.

Singing I become my song until
death drowns my cry.
Dark cuts the sun down as the season wills.
Nothing lives long, But the earth and the hills —

Joanna Cattonar

Villanelle for the Spiders

The smallest weavers work at night
To link together all they know
And build their web that holds our light.

It's drops of dew that catch my sight
And tell me, when through dawn I go,
That smallest weavers work at night.

I find the spiral fabric slight
And wonder how they spin so slow
Yet build their web that holds our light.

A touch could tear, my deep breath might
Destroy the net their trust put low,
For smallest weavers work at night.

Patience is life and their delight,
Ready again if wind should blow
To build their web that holds our light.

Our feeble threads are strung so tight
Across the darkness deep below.
The smallest weavers work at night
To build their web that holds our light.

                    Kim Stafford

Missouri Woods

Post oak, white oak, black oak, Ozark rails,
shake roofs and fences split with maul and froe:
remember the timberland, the vanished trails.

Laid, lapped and panelled, propped or locked with nails,
the zigzag fences stretching row on row =
post oak, white oak, black oak, Ozark rails.

Tables and staves and dishes, pitch-lined pails
curled from a blade and fashioned long ago,
remember the timberland, the vanished trails.

Cradles and coffins, rafts loaded with bales,
bolts, blocks and pickets, handles for hammer and hoe;
post oak, white oak, black oak, Ozark rails,

logs hollowed for john boats, poles for paddles and sails =
their stubble and stumps poke up the crusted snow.
(remember the timberland, the vanished trails?)

The blown out nest, the branch that cracks and fails
are lost from the land where only the birds know.
Post oak, white oak, black oak, Ozark rails,
remember the timberland, the vanished trails.

                    Charles Guenther

Runes for an Old Believer

The wolves of evening will be much abroad =
Hold to the sprig of rowan
When we are near the evening of the world.

The weather darkens; wilderness and wood
Thicken with stalkers; when the sun goes down,
The wolves of evening will be much abroad.

They creep toward fold and barn, across the field,
Gaunt-gray or shagbark-brown,
When we are near the evening of the world.

The herd their meat, their smell the smell of blood,

The ground their ground, the bolted house their own,
The wolves of evening will be much abroad.

The body, like the oak, is bent and gnarled,
The shallow-rooted mind is overthrown,
When we are near the evening of the world.

If iron fails, and salt, and Aaron's rod,
Hold to the twig of rowan.
When we are near the evening of the world,
The wolves of evening will be much abroad.

Rolfe Humphries

Canticle for Xmas Eve

O holy night as it was in the beginning
Under silent stars for the butchering of sheep
And shepherds, is now and ever shall be, night,

How still we see thee lying under the angels
In twisted wreckage, squealing, each empty eye-slit
Brimful of light as it was in the beginning

Of our slumber through the sirens wailing and keening
Over the stained ax and the shallow grave
That was, is now, and ever shall be, night

Of the night-light, chain and deadlatch by the bolt
Slammed home, the spell of thy deep and dreamless
Everlasting sleep as it was in the beginning

Of the bursting forth of bright arterial blossoms
From the pastures of our hearts to the dark streets
Shining what is and shall be for this night

Of bludgeons and hopes, of skulls and fears laid open
To the mercies of our fathers burning in heaven,
O little town of bedlam in the beginning
Of the end as it was, as it is to all, good night.

David Wagoner

Home Movies

Tumbling with sticks of particled light
the grainy faces of a buried summer
reel again, boneless on a white

patch of wall whose edges slide,
cannot frame us as we shimmer

through ruins whose particled light

jostles the sudden flight
of hills, a forgotten manor, stammer
of old sky & the bone-white

wave of a hand that died
five years ago this summer
as we sit in particled light

watching ourselves as we might
have been, the too-fluent grammar
of forgotten gestures boneless on a white

patch of wall, knowing this cannot be right:
that only the pose is what matters
    & not what came after,
the tumbling with sticks of particled light,
unreal again, sudden patch of boneless white.

Barbara Lefcowitz

Rerun Berries
A Prose Villanelle

The island will be the same, prearranged like a cheese platter,
wired flowers, the choreography of a campfire: fear of the known
& expected. Yet there is a double possiblity in all repetitions
& returns: the threat of boredom, the lure of entering your own
reopened gestures, wearing them as if nothing had happened since
you zippered them shut & folded their gestures aside. Far from
least lurks the challenge of those lines written last summer as
we left: "if I return to that island/the rerun berries will be
soured by memory/the inevitable comparison with this summer's
fluent hoard."

Things are not exactly the same: rabbit skin missing from
outhouse door; jug with cracked lip missing from kitchen; because
of unchary winter, growth cycle out of phase — few raspberries,
many wild iris. Uneasily I curve into the contours of last
summer's favorite posture, a semifoetal curl on the tower room's
pillowed ledge; feel as if I am watching myself in a crudely shot
home movie. So the island will not be the same, the
prearrangement with its forced analogies of cheese platter, wired
flowers, & campfire choreography was merely a verbal trick to
divert from my fear of disappointment, fear of the unexpected &
unknown.

Shred the script of self-parody, scatter it between the strings
of wild grass even as the wind shapes its sway, scatter it over
the ocean's moon-tugged sameness. In the cove gulls quote &

requote their sparsely musicked syllables, seaweed quotes its
frailty. I have returned to the island, but will not recover
last summer's raspberry swales, will have to bucket another red
fluency, uproot the artifacts of a different hoard.

The bone china moon that displays itself on last summer's shelf
of sky: is it the identical moon or a clone? The blood that
spurts from my brambled skin: is it the same blood that wined
last summer's ceremonial wording or a cunning facsimile? The
island whose prearrangement I likened to a cheese platter, wired
flowers, the choreography of a campfire: is it still what I need
to know?

There are many eyes in the tower room: eyes of pine in the wall
slats; eyes that pan the ceaselessly changing sameness of the
ocean; eyes that see my predecessor sprawled on this same ledge,
panning the ceaselessly changing sameness of the ocean. But her
eyes are blind to my presence as the eyes in a photograph, as
ignorant of what separates us as I am ignorant of what I will
dream tonight; the physiognymy of my great-grandchildren; the
taste of next October's apples. By returning to Ragged Island, I
have learned the catechism of return: memory itself is the
fluent & expanding hoard, season it as you will.

Twice is repetition, three times or more will be ritual. Spread
the roughly grassed cloth, break out the dancing masks! Next
summer the island will be more or less the same, prearranged like
a platter of wild stones, tangled swamp candles, the choreography
of a forest fire: fear neither the known or the unexpected.
When I return to this island, the rerun berries will enter the
blood jam of memory, joining me to my unknowable successor,
joining this & last summer's fluent hoard.

Barbara F. Lefcowitz

Notes

Chapter 1.
The Italian Villanella and the Problems of "Popular Art"

1. Bianca Maria Galanti, *Le Villanelle alla napolitana* (Florence: Leo Olschki, 1954): 22–23. Subsequent references to this and other sources will be made in the text after initial annotation.

2. Gennaro Maria Monti, *Le Villanelle* (Castello: Il Solco, 1925): 36.

3. Carlo Calcaterra, "Canzoni villanesche e villanelle," *Archivum Romanicum* 10 (1926): 264.

4. Galanti, xxxii–iii. Galanti surveys the controversy over the "popular" status of the form beginning with Mario Menghini's "Villanelle alla Napolitana," *Zeitschrift für Romanische Philologie*, 16, 17 (1892–93): 476–503, 441–89.

5. Calcaterra, 272–47, Alfred Einstein, *The Italian Madrigal, 1 (Princeton: University Press, 1949):* 344.

6. Galanti, xxxiii.

7. Monti, 196. The Portugese vilançete is virtually identical in form and content to the Spanish villancico. *See*, for example, Garcia de Resende, *Cancioneiro geral* (Coimbra: University Press, 1910–1917), 5 vols.; and Pierre Le Gentil, *La Poesie lyrique espagnole et portugaise a la fin du moyen age* (Rennes: Plihon, 1949), 2 vols.

8. Antonio Sánchez Romeralo, *El Villancico* (Madrid: Biblioteca Romanánica Hispanica, 1969): 50.

9. Thomás Navarro, *Métrica Española* (Syracuse: University Press, 1956): 535. Navarro traces the form from its origins as a *cantiga de estribillo* and in the zéjel, through the Renaissance, *Siglo de Oro*, the Neoclassic Period, to the Postmodern era.

10. D. Rafael Mitjana, ed., *Cincuenta y Cuatro del Siglo XVI* (Uppsala: Almqvist, 1909): 19.

11. Gerald Brenan, *The Literature of the Spanish People*, 2nd ed. (Cambridge: University Press, 1976): 121.

12. Giuseppe Guido Ferrero, ed., *Marino e i Marinisti* (Milan: Riccardo Ricciardi, n.d.): 758.

13. Alfredo Obertello, "Villanelle e Madrigali Inediti in Inghilterra," *Italian Studies* 3 (1947–48): 131–144.

14. Orlando di Lasso, *Sämtliche Werke*, vol. 10 (New York: Broude Brothers, 1973; rpr. of Leipzig, 1898 ed.): n.p.

15. C. M. Bowra, *Primitive Song* (Cleveland: World, 1962): 28–29, 34–35, 47.

16. Galanti, xxvii.

17. Everett Helm, "Secular Vocal Music in Italy (c. 1400–1530)," *New Oxford History of Music* 3 (London: Oxford University Press, 1960): 383.

18. Einstein, 60.

19. E. J. Dent, "The Sixteenth-Century Madrigal," *New Oxford History of Music* 4 (London: Oxford University Press, 1968): 53.

20. Monti, 292–94; Galanti, xxiv.

21. Beckman C. Cannon, Alvin H. Johnson, William G. Waite, *The Art of Music* (New York: Thomas Y. Crowell, 1960): 189. This text includes an analysis of Marenzio's madrigal emphasizing the "literary" treatment by the musician of the poetic text.

22. Gustave Reese, *Music in the Renaissance*, rev. ed. (New York: Norton, 1959): 444–45.

Chapter 2.
The Villanelle in Sixteenth-Century French Poetry

1. Gennaro Maria Monti, *Le Villanelle* (Castello: Il Solco, 1925): 207.

2. Melin de Saint-Gelais, *Oeuvres poétiques* 2 (Paris: Paul Duffis, 1878): 230–33.

3. Warner Forrest Patterson, *French Poetic Theory*, Part IV (Ann Arbor: University of Michigan, 1935): 380.

4. Joachim Du Bellay, *Oeuvres poétiques* 5 (Paris: Librarire Huchette, 1923): 16.

5. Étienne Jodelle, *Oeuvres complètes*, I (Paris: Gallimard, 1965): 318–19.

6. Philippe Desportes, *Oeuvres* (Paris: Adolphe Delahays, 1858): 395.

7. Jean Palerne, *Poésies* (Geneva: Slatkine Reprints, 1971; rpr. of Paris 1884 ed.): 115.

8. Pierre Blanchemain, ed., "Jean Passerat, sa vie et ses oeuvres," *Les Poésies françaises* 1 (Geneva: Slatkine Reprints, 1968; rpr. of Paris 1880 ed.): vii. Citations of Passerat's poems refer to this edition.

9. Monti, 49.

10. Patterson, Part I, 58.

11. Some anticipation of how the villanelle was to be received into English poetry at the end of the nineteenth century can be gained by reflecting upon John Payne's translation of Passerat's concluding couplet: "I have lost my turlte-doo;/After her I'd fain ensue." No such stilted cuteness is required by the French original. In Huntington Cairns, ed., *The Limits of Art* (Washington, D.C.: Pantheon, 1948): 539.

12. Honoré D'Urfé, *L'Astrée* 1 (Lyon: Pierre Masson, 1925): 200. *See* Monti, 147 ff. for his account of similar contexts in Giambattista Basile's *Pentamerone*.

Chapter 3.
The Revival of a "Poetical Trifle"

1. George Saintsbury, *A Short History of French Literature*, 7th ed. (Oxford: Clarendon, 1918): 182.

2. Pierre de Ronsard, *Oeuvres complètes* 2 (Paris: Gallimard, 1966): 390.

3. George Pellisier, ed., *L'Art poétique de Vauquelin* (Paris: Garnier, 1885): 40–41.

4. La Sieur De la Croix, *L'Art poésie françoise et latine* (Lyon: Thomas Amaulry, 1694): 331.

5. *See*, for example, the *Reflexions sur la poésie* (1734) by R.D.S.M.; M. Domairon's *Poétique française* (1804); Auguste Carion's *Enseignement méthodique de la versification française*, 4th ed. (1859); L. Quicherat's *Traité de la versification française*, 2nd ed. (1850); and Gustave Weigand's *Traité de versification française* (1863).

6. Auguste Carion, *Enseignement*, 4th ed. (Paris: P. Lethielleux, 1859): 76.

7. Gustave Weigand, *Traité* (Bromberg: Louis Levit, 1863): 147.

8. Philippe Martinon, *Les Strophes* (Paris: Honore Champion, 1911): 80. Despite allusions to Banville, Rollinat, and Leconte de Lisle, all of whom wrote villanelles, Martinon does not mention the villanelle.

9. Clair Tisseur, *Modestes observations sur l'art de versifier* (Lyon: Bernaux et Cumin, 1893): 317.

10. L. E. Kastner, *A History of French Versification* (Oxford: Clarendon, 1903): 279-281.

11. Warner Forrest Patterson, *Three Centuries of French Poetic Theory* 1 (Ann Arbor: University of Michigan Press, 1935): 222. Volume 14 of the series University of Michigan Publications in Language and Literature.

12. Charles Le Goffic and Édouard Thieulin, in *Nouveau traité de versification française*, 4th ed. (Paris: Masson, 1903): 149, recognize Philoxène Boyer as resuscitator of Passerat's form. But Boyer's "La Marquise Aurore" was published in *Les Deux saisons* in 1867, some ten years after Banville's poem appeared in *Odes funambulesques* and more than twenty years after it was written. Boyer collaborated with Banville on two verse dramas in 1853 and 1857.

13. Théophile Gautier, *Poésies complètes* 2 (Paris: Firmin-Didot, 1932): 208.

14. Joachim Du Bellay, *Oeuvres poétiques* 5 (Paris: Hachette, 1923): 27-28.

15. *See*, for example, Charles Aubertin, *La Versification française et ses nouveaux théoriciens* (Paris: Belin, 1898): 269-270, and Gaëtan Hecq and Louis Paris, *La Poétique française* (Paris: Émile Bouillon, 1896): 278-79. This view is not universally shared, however. *See also* L.E. Kastner, *History*, 280.

16. Théodore de Banville, *Poésies complètes* 1 (Paris: Charpentier, 1878): 146. Originally appeared in *Odes funambulesques* (1857).

17. Théodore de Banville, *Petit traité de poésie française* (Paris: Charpentier, 1898): 215.

18. Philoxène Boyer, *Les Deux saisons* (Paris: Alphonse Lemeurre, 1867), as quoted in Banville, *Petit traité* (n17 above): 214.

19. Théodore de Banville, *Les Camées parisiens*, Troisième et Derniere Série (Geneva: Slatkine Reprints, 1970; rpr. of Paris eds. 1866-73): 34.

20. Joseph Boulmier, *Villanelles* (Paris: I. Liseux, 1878): 14.

21. *See* Andrew Lang, "Villanelle: To M. Joseph Boulmier," *Ballads and Rhymes* (London: Longmans, 1911): 171. Originally published in *Rhymes á la Mode* (1884).

22. W. E. Henley, *Works* 2 (London: David Nutt, 1908): 228. Originally published in *Book of Verses* (1888).

23. Ernest Dowson, *Poems*, 5th ed. (London: John Lane, 1913): 52. Originally published in August, 1893.

24. Personal interview with James Dickey conducted in Moscow, Idaho at the University of Idaho, 26 April 1979.

25. Jerome Beaty and William H. Matchett, *Poetry: From Statement to Meaning* (New York: Oxford, 1965): 149.

26. Leconte de Lisle, *Oeuvres* 3 (Paris: Société d'Édition, 1977): 37.

27. Maurice Rollinat, *Les Névroses* (Paris: Charpentier, 1910): 270-72.

28. Henri Morier, *Dictionnaire de poétique et de rhétorique* (Paris: Presses Universitaires, 1961): 468.

29. Maurice Rollinat, *La Nature* (Paris: Charpentier, 1892): 278.

30. *See* E. A. Robinson, *Collected Poems* (New York: Macmillan, 1954): 80-81. "The House on the Hill" and "Villanelle of Change" were first published in *The Globe* (1894) and *Harvard Advocate* (1891).

Chapter 4.
The Villanelle in English: 1874-1922

1. James K. Robinson, "A Neglected Phase of the Aesthetic Movement: English Parnassianism," *PMLA* 68 (September 1953): 754.

2. Robinson, 738.

3. Robinson, 754.

4. See Philip K. Jason's "Modern Versions of the Villanelle," *College Literature* 7 (Spring 1980): 136-145.

5. Théodore de Banville, *Petite traité de poésie française* (Paris: Charpentier, 1898): 215.

6. Edmund W. Gosse, "A Plea for Certain Exotic Forms of Verse," *Cornhill Magazine* 36 (1877): 53-72.

7. Calvin S. Brown, *Music and Literature* (Athens: University of Georgia Press, 1968; rpr. of 1948 ed.): 147-48.

8. Brander Matthews, *A Study of Versification* (Boston: Houghton Mifflin, 1911): 158.

9. Austin Dobson, *Collected Poems*, 9th ed. (London: Kegan Paul, 1913): 482. In his notes (p. 667), Dobson dates his villanelles from 1877.

10. Mary J. J. Wrinn, *The Hollow Reed* (New York: Harper, 1935): 229.

11. Austin Dobson, *Miscellanies, Second Series* (New York: AMS,

1970; rpr. of London 1901 ed): 206.

12. Dobson, *Collected Poems*, 184.

13. Oscar Wilde, "Pan—A Villanelle," quoted in Helen Louise Cohen's *Lyric Forms from France* (New York: Harcourt, 1922): 425. This poem was parodied by "Frank Danby." *See* Francis Winwar (Grebanier), *Oscar Wilde and the Yellow 'Nineties* (New York: Harper, 1940): 59–60.

14. Oscar Wilde, *First Collected Edition* (London: Dawsons, 1969): 158.

15. *See* A. S. F. Gow's edition of the idylls and epigrams, *Theocritus*, I, 2nd ed. (Cambridge: University Press, 1965): 49–51. Notes, *Theocritus*, II, p. 92.

16. Andrew Lang, *Ballades & Rhymes* (London: Longmans, 1911): 98–99.

17. Raymond M. Alden, *English Verse* (New York: Henry Holt, 1903): 377. *See also* Clarence E. Andrews, *The Writing and Reading of Verse* (New York: Appleton, 1918): 249; and Henri Morier, *Dictionnaire de poétique et de rhétorique* (Paris: Presses Universitaires, 1961): 468.

18. W. E. Henley, *Works* 2 (London: David Nutt, 1908): 227.

19. Matthews, 158.

20. Carolyn Wells, ed., *A Whimsey Anthology* (New York: Scribner's, 1906): 162–63.

21. *See* Elizabeth Aslin, *The Aesthetic Movement* (New York: Praeger, 1969): Plate 58. The illustration shows a dining room in Morris wallpaper and lined with blue china.

22. In a letter of July 1892, Wilde describes Henley as "too coarse, too offensive, too personal, to be sent any work of mine." Rupert Hart-Davis, ed., *Letters of Oscar Wilde* (New York: Harcourt, 1962): 318.

23. Frances Winwar (Grebanier), *Oscar Wilde and the Yellow 'Nineties* (New York: Harper, 1940): 26.

24. *The Life of Oscar Wilde*, anonymous compilation (New York: Lamb, 1909): 49.

25. Vyvyan Holland, *Oscar Wilde: A Pictorial Biography* (New York: Viking, 1960): 34. I am indebted to Prof. Karl Beckson of Brooklyn College, CUNY, for guiding me to this volume and for straightening out my initial reading of Henley's poem.

26. John Davidson, *In a Music Hall* (London: Ward & Downey, 1891): 26–27.

27. Ernest Dowson, *Peoms*, 5th ed. (London: John Lane, 1913): 52–53.

28. James Whitcomb Riley, *Complete Poetical Works* (New York: Grosset & Dunlap, 1937): 296–97.

29. The anthology, *Verses from the Harvard Advocate*, Third Series 1886–1906 (Cambridge: Harvard Advocate, 1906), does not include Robinson's "Villanelle of Change," but it does include (p. 8) one by Mark Antony DeWolfe Howe, Jr. of the class of 1887.

30. E. A. Robinson, *Collected Poems* (New York: Macmillan, 1954): 80–81. These villanelles also appeared in *The Torrent*, published privately the year before *Children of the Night*.

31. Richard Cary, *Early Reception of Edwin Arlington Robinson* (Waterville: Colby college Press, 1974): 55, 238. Subsequent references to early reviews of Robinson's work are to this useful, annotated edition and are included in the text.

32. E. A. Robinson, *Untriangulated Stars* (Cambridge: Harvard University Press, 1947): 132. Cited in text as *Letters*.

33. Cary, 42. Readers have sometimes been unconvinced. Louis Coxe, in *Edwin Arlington Robinson* (New York: Pegasus, 1969): 42, insists that there is some connection between the decaying house and the disintegration of Robinson's family, particularly of his addicted brother.

Chapter 5.
From Ezra Pound to Mid-Century:
The Form in a Major Key

1. Ezra Pound, *Literary Essays* (New York: New Directions, 1968): 369n.

2. K. K. Ruthven, *A Guide to Ezra Pound's Personae* (Berkeley: University of California, 1969): 242. *See also* Peter Brooker, *A Student's Guide to the Selected Poems of Ezra Pound* (London: Faber, 1979): 108.

3. Ezra Pound, *Personae* (New York: New Directions, 1950): 158–59.

4. William Empson, *Collected Poems* (New York: Harcourt, 1949): 23.

5. Philip and Averil Gardner, *The God Approached* (London: Chatto, 1978): 90.

6. Helen Louise Cohen, *Lyric Forms from France* (New York: Harcourt, 1922): 416. "Villanelle at Verona" is not included in Dobson's *Collected Poems*, 9th ed. (London: Kegan Paul, 1913). Cohen's volume is the largest collection of villanelles in English to the present.

7. Ernest Dowson, *Poems*, 5th ed. (London: John Lane, 1913): 52.

8. W. H. Auden, *Collected Poems* (New York: Random, 1976): 244–45.

9. John Fuller, *A Reader's Guide to W. H. Auden* (New York: Farrar, 1970): 180. From an anonymous review in *Vice Versa* (Jan./Feb. 1941).

10. Auden, 243–44.

11. Louise Baughan Murdy, *Sound and Sense in Dylan Thomas's Poetry* (The Hague: Mouton, 1966): 96.

12. William York Tindall, *A Reader's Guide to Dylan Thomas* (New York: Noonday, 1962): 204.

13. David Holbrook, *Dylan Thomas: The Code of Night* (London: Athlone, 1972): 196.

14. Holbrook, 196.

15. Ernest Becker, *The Denial of Death* (New York: Free Press, 1973): 11.

16. Karl Malkoff, *Theodore Roethke* (New York: Columbia, 1966): 123.

17. Malkoff, 122.

18. Theodore Roethke, *Collected Poems* (New York: Doubleday, 1966): 108.

19. Jenijoy LaBelle, *The Echoing Wood of Theodore Roethke* (Princeton: University Press, 1976): 109.

20. Malkoff, 218, 219.

21. Roethke, 250.

22. Lois Ames, "Notes Toward a Biography," in Charles Newman, ed., *The Art of Sylvia Plath* (Bloomington: Indiana University Press, 1970): 162.

23. Sylvia Plath, "Mad Girl's Love Song," *Mademoiselle* 37 (August 1953): 358.

24. Edward Butscher, *Sylvia Plath: Method and Madness* (New York: Seabury Press, 1976): 74.

25. Richard Eberhart, *Collected Poems* (New York: Oxford, 1976): 184. First published in *Spectrum* (Winter 1957).

26. Richard Ellmann and Robert O'Clair, *The Norton Anthology of Modern Poetry* (New York: Norton, 1973): 661.

27. Donald Justice, "Preface," *The Collected Poems of Weldon Kees* (Lincoln: University of Nebraska, 1975): vii. Henceforth cited as "Kees."

28. Kees, 65.

29. Kees, 67–68.

30. Kees, 68.

31. Lew Welch, *Ring of Bone: Collected Poems 1950–1971* (Bolinas, CA: Grey Fox Press, 1979): 60, 61.

32. Gary Snyder, *Left Out in the Rain* (San Francisco: North Point Press, 1986): 181.

33. There is, in fact, at least one villanelle in Scottish dialect: Margaret Winfride Simpson's "O Winter Wind, Lat Grievin Be," in *The Oxford Book of Scottish Verse* (Oxford: Clarendon, 1966): 483–84.

Chapter 6.
The Form and its Transformation
in Contemporary Poetry

1. William Empson, *Collected Poems* (New York: Harcourt, 1949): 23.

2. Theodore Roethke, *Collected Poems* (New York: Doubleday, 1966): 108.

3. Sylvia Plath, "Mad Girl's Love Song," *Mademoiselle* 37 (August 1953): 358.

4. Joseph Langland, "The Green Town: Poems," in *Poets of Today* 3 (New York: Scribner's, 1956): 144.

5. Barbara Howes, "The Triumph of Death," in Rolfe Humphries, ed., *New Poems by American Poets* 2 (New York: Ballantine, 1957): 77.

6. James Merrill, *Water Street* (New York: Atheneum, 1967): 27.

7. The Black Mountain College poets, the followers of Charles Olson's "Projective" or "Open" verse, have been partially responsible for this renewed interest in the appearance of the poem on the page, and certainly e. e. cummings's experiments in typography are a part of it. That this interest is a "renewal" is evident to anyone who knows such poems of the seventeenth century as George Herbert's "Easter-Wings" or Thomas Traherne's *Thanksgivings*.

8. Marilyn Hacker, Correspondence with me dated 27 January 1978.

9. Marilyn Hacker, *Presentation Piece* (New York: Viking, 1974): 89.

10. Marilyn Hacker, *Separations* (New York: Knopf, 1976): 57.

11. Hacker, *Presentation Piece*, 43.

12. Rachel Hadas, Correspondence with me dated 24 March 1978.

13. Rachel Hadas, "Pale Cast," *The Harvard Advocate* 11 (October 1976).

14. Gilbert Sorrentino, *The Perfect Fiction* (New York: Norton, 1968): 36.

15. Richard Hugo, Correspondence with me dated 27 October 1978.

16. Richard Hugo, *What Thou Lovest Well, Remains American* (New York: Norton, 1975): 46.

17. William Pitt Root, "Terrorist from the Heartland," unpublished.

18. William Pitt Root, *The Storm* (New York: Atheneum, 1969).

19. Karen Swenson, "I Have Lost the Address of My Country," *Prairie Schooner* 51 (Spring 1983): 69.

20. Denise Levertov, *With Eyes at the Back of Our Heads* (New York: New Directions, 1959): 20. Levertov has noted, however, that "Form exists only *in* the content and language." Of her tercets, she observes that, given the dynamic nature of composition, such stanzas constitute "a regularity of pattern that looks like, but is not, predetermined." *See* Donald Allen and Warren Tallman, ed., *The Poetics of the New American Poetry* (New York: Grove, 1973): 310, 315.

21. Barbara Lefcowitz, Correspondence with me dated 30 March 1978.

22. Judith Johnson Sherwin, *How the Dead Count* (New York: Norton, 1978): 62.

23. Sherwin, p. 48. Lefcowitz, two villanelles in *Song*, 3/4 (1977): 4, 5.

24. Christopher Millis, "Ceremony," *Cutbank* 26 (Spring/Summer 1986): 16.

Appendix A. The Villanelle and the Poet

1. Marjorie Boulton, *The Anatomy of Poetry* (London: Routledge, 1953): 143.

2. "Announcements," *Coda* 5 (April/May 1978): 30.

3. Imogene Bolls, Correspondence, 28 June 1978. Correspondents will be annotated only upon the first citation.

4. Carol Poster, Correspondence, 4 April 1979.

5. Jon Daunt, Correspondence, 28 May 1978.

6. Grace Morton, Correspondence, 27 July 1978.

7. Helen Saslow, Correspondence, 11 April 1978.

8. Barbara Lefcowitz, Correspondence, 30 March 1978.

9. Alberto Ríos, Correspondence, 8 April 1978.

10. Joanne Seltzer, Correspondence, 28 March 1978.

11. Mary J. J. Wrinn, *The Hollow Reed* (New York: Harper, 1935): 278-290.

12. Harold Bond, Correspondence, 10 May 1978.

13. Billie Jean James, Correspondence, June 1978.

14. James Dickey, Interview, University of Idaho, 26 April 1979.

15. Sanford Pinsker, Correspondence, undated.

16. Marilyn Folkestad, Correspondence, 19 March 1979.

17. Philip Dacey, Correspondence, 14 April 1978.

18. Harald Wyndham, Correspondence, 8 April 1978.

19. Annette Hayn, Correspondence, 27 April 1978.

20. Theodore Hall, Correspondence, 18 April 1978.

21. Dorothy Foltz-Gray, Correspondence, undated.

22. Joanna Cattonar, Correspondence, 4 May 1978.

23. Duane Carr, Correspondence, 26 April 1978.

24. George Keithley, Correspondence, 16 June 1978.

25. Grace Morton, "Leopards and the Artist," *Mississippi Review*.

Index

fin de siécle, 65, 70
Folkestad, Marilyn, 114, 132
Foltz-Gray, Dorothy, 114
Fresnaye, Vauquelin de la, 44
Frost, Robert, x
frottola, 3, 19, 20
Fuller, John, 150

Galanti, Bianca Maria, 2, 6, 11, 12, 16, 17
Gardner, Philip and Averil, 86
Gautier, Théophile, 46, 47
Goffic, Charles Le, 146
Gosse, Edmund, 61–66, 69, 70, 72, 73, 76, 80
Grévin, Jacques, 43
Guenther, Charles, 138
Gummere, Francis B., 76

Hacker, Marilyn, 60, 100–103, 116
Hadas, Rachel, 102, 103
Hall, Theodore, 114, 115, 127
Harkness, Edward, 132
Hart-Davis, Rupert, 148
Hayn, Annette, 114, 128
Hecq, Gaëtan, 146
Helm, Everett, 19
Henley, W. E., 50, 51, 58, 59, 61, 70, 71, 73, 76, 77, 148
Herbert, George, 90, 98, 151
Herrick, Robert, 70
Hirsch, Bonnie, 127
Holbrook, David, 89
Holland, Vyvyan, 148
Howes, Barbara, 98
Hughes, Langston, 80
Hugo, Richard, 60, 105
Humphries, Rolfe, 139

image(-ry, -istic), 8, 10, 11, 13–19, 38, 64, 90
irony(-ic), 15, 40, 47, 55, 91, 101

Jacob, Max, 60
James, Billie Jean, 113
Janowitz, Phyllis, 134

Morier, Henri, 58, 147
Morton, Grace, 112, 115
mudanza, 3
Murdy, Louise Baughan, 88

Nasco, Giovanni, 14
Nauwach, Johann, 24
Navarro, Thomas, 143
Neapolitan, 1, 2, 6, 9, 13, 15, 21
Nemerov, Howard, 136
Nola, Giovanni da, 2, 11, 16, 20, 21

Obertello, Alfredo, 7, 13-15
Olson, Charles, 151
O'Neill, Eugene, ix
ottava rima, 7, 33

Packard, William, 130
Palerne, Jean, 34, 37
paradox(-ical), x, 11, 15, 32, 37, 38, 88-92, 94, 99, 103
Paris, Louis, 146
Parnassian(s), 49, 61
Parsons, James C., 76
Partridge, Eric, 71
Passerat, Jean, x, 1, 7, 27, 30-33, 35-37, 40, 41, 43-46, 48, 49, 53,
        54, 56, 58, 62-64, 76, 103, 104, 116, 145, 146
Patterson, Warner Forrest, 27, 29, 36, 45
Payne, John, 61, 80, 145
Perissone, Cambio, 2
Petrarch, Francis, 5, 13, 16, 23
Petrarchan, 1, 7-9, 14-16, 40
Petrarchism, 3, 13, 16
Petroski, Henry, 131
Pinsker, Sanford, 113, 114
Plath, Sylvia, 60, 88, 92, 93, 97, 116
Pléiade, 27, 28, 31, 37, 43, 44, 46, 48
Poe, Edgar Allan, 56, 59
poesia per musica, 2, 8, 23
Poster, Carol, 112, 113
Pound, Ezra, 60, 75, 80, 83-85, 87, 89, 96, 104, 116
précieuse(-x), 37, 54

Regnart, Jakob, 24
Renaissance, x, 4, 13, 43, 46, 47, 66, 80
Resende, Garcia de, 143
Rhymers' Club, 73
Riley, James Whitcomb, 76, 77
rima alternata, 6, 27
rima bacciata, 6, 14, 19, 28, 35
rima incrociata, 6, 27, 32
Rios, Alberto, 112, 121, 135
Roberts, Walter Adolphe, 80
Robinson, Edwin Arlington, 59, 60, 77–80, 109, 116, 149
Robinson, James K., 61
Roethke, Theodore, x, xiv, 52, 60, 80, 88, 90–92, 96, 97, 99, 103, 109, 111, 116
Rollinat, Maurice, 45, 56–59. 63, 104
Romeralo, Antonio Sánchez, 3–5, 10, 17
Ronsard, Pierre de, 27, 28, 43, 145
Roosevelt, Theodore, 78
Root, William Pitt, 106, 107
Rossetti, Dante Gabriel, 71
Ruthven, K. K., 83

Saint-Gelais, Melin de, 27, 29, 43
Saintsbury, George, 43
Sand, George, 56
Saslow, Helen, 112, 114, 125
Scollard, Clinton, 80
Seltzer, Joanne, 112
Sempronio, Giovan Leone, 6
Sherwin, Judith Johnson, 108, 109
Simpson, Margaret Winfride, 151
Skeat, W. W., ix, 80
Smith, Henry DeForest, 79
Snow, Herbert, 66
sonnet, ix, x, 6, 52, 61, 76
Sorrentino, Gilbert, 60, 104, 105, 112, 116
Stafford, Kim, 138
Stevick, Philip, 108, 116
strambotto, 7, 19
Swenson, Karen, 107
Symbolist, 61
Symons, Arthur, 73

RICKS COLLEGE
DAVID O. McKAY LIBRARY
REXBURG, IDAHO 83440